JAZZ/ROCK HORN SECTION

CONTENTS

Transcribed by Forrest "Woody" Mankowski

ISBN 978-1-61780-475-5

7777 W. Bluemound Rd. P.O. Box 13819 Milwaukee, WI 53213

Visit Hal Leonard Online at
www.halleonard.com

AND WHEN I DIE

Words and Music by
LAURA NYRO

11
A6
D6
A6
D6
A6
D6
A6
D6
don't real - ly care.
If it's peace you find in dy - in', well then,
Tpt. 1,2,3.
Alto Sax
Tenor Sax
Tbn. 1,2.

Almost Double-Time 𝅗𝅥 = 112
15
E9sus
D6
A6
G
D
let the time be near.
If it's peace you find in dy - in', and if dy -
Tpt. 1,2,3.
Alto Sax
Tenor Sax
Tbn. 1,2.

19
G
D
E7sus
Bm7
C♯m7
D6
E9sus
- in' time is near,___ just bun - dle up___ my___ cof - fin, 'cause it's
Tpt. 1,2,3.
Alto Sax
Tenor Sax
Tbn. 1,2.

To Coda 𝄌
23
A6
D6
A6
D6
A6
D6
A6
cold way down_ there, I hear_ that it's cold way down_ there, yeah,___
Tpt. 1,2,3.
Alto Sax
Tenor Sax
Tbn. 1,2.

27
D6
C♯m7
Bm7
E9sus
A
D
A
D
cra - zy cold way down there.
And when I
Tpt. 1,2,3.
Alto Sax
Tenor Sax
Tbn. 1,2.

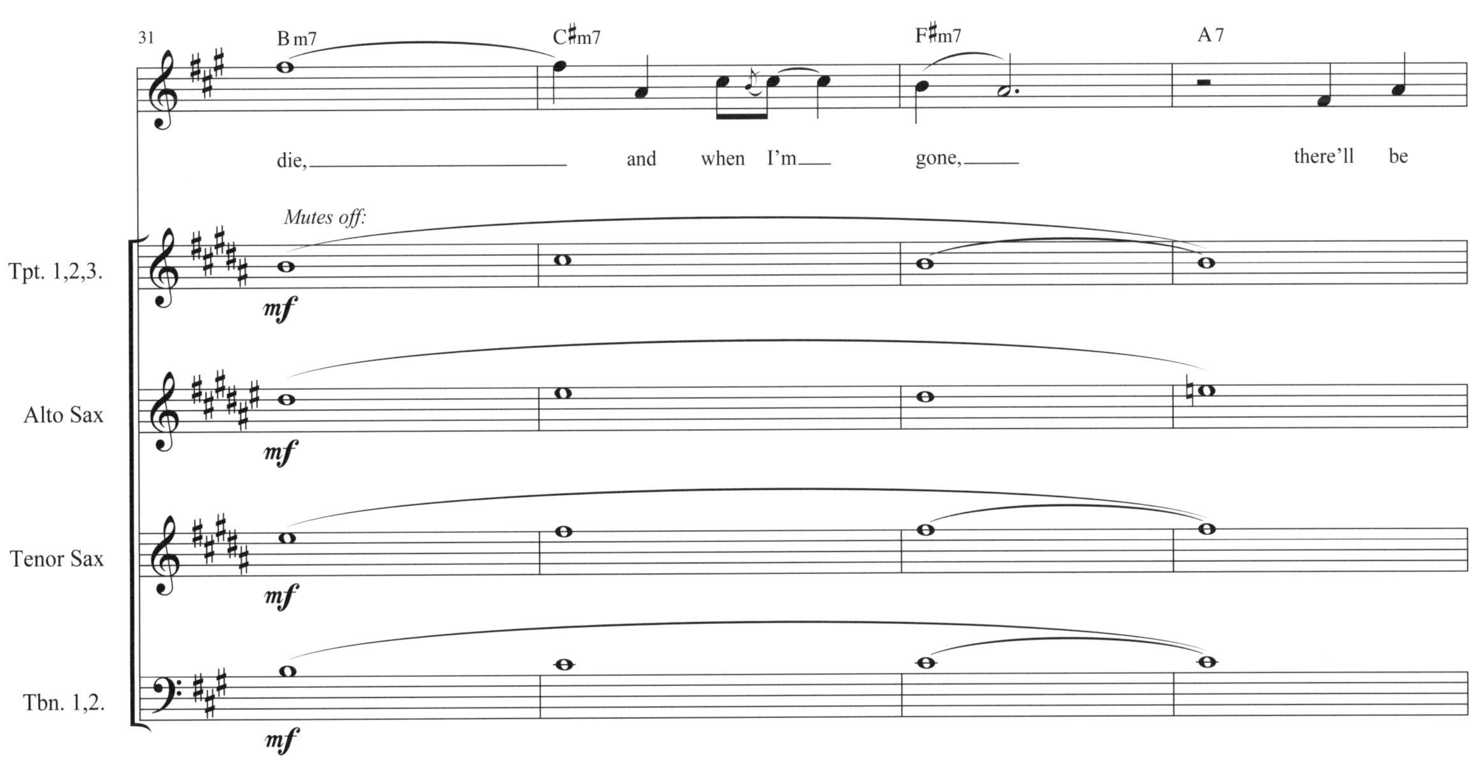
31
Bm7
C♯m7
F♯m7
A7
die, and when I'm gone, there'll be
Mutes off:
mf
Tpt. 1,2,3.
Alto Sax
Tenor Sax
Tbn. 1,2.

35
D
C♯m
Bm7
E9sus
one child born in this world to car - ry on, to car - ry on.
Tpt. 1,2,3.
Alto Sax
Tenor Sax
Tbn. 1,2.

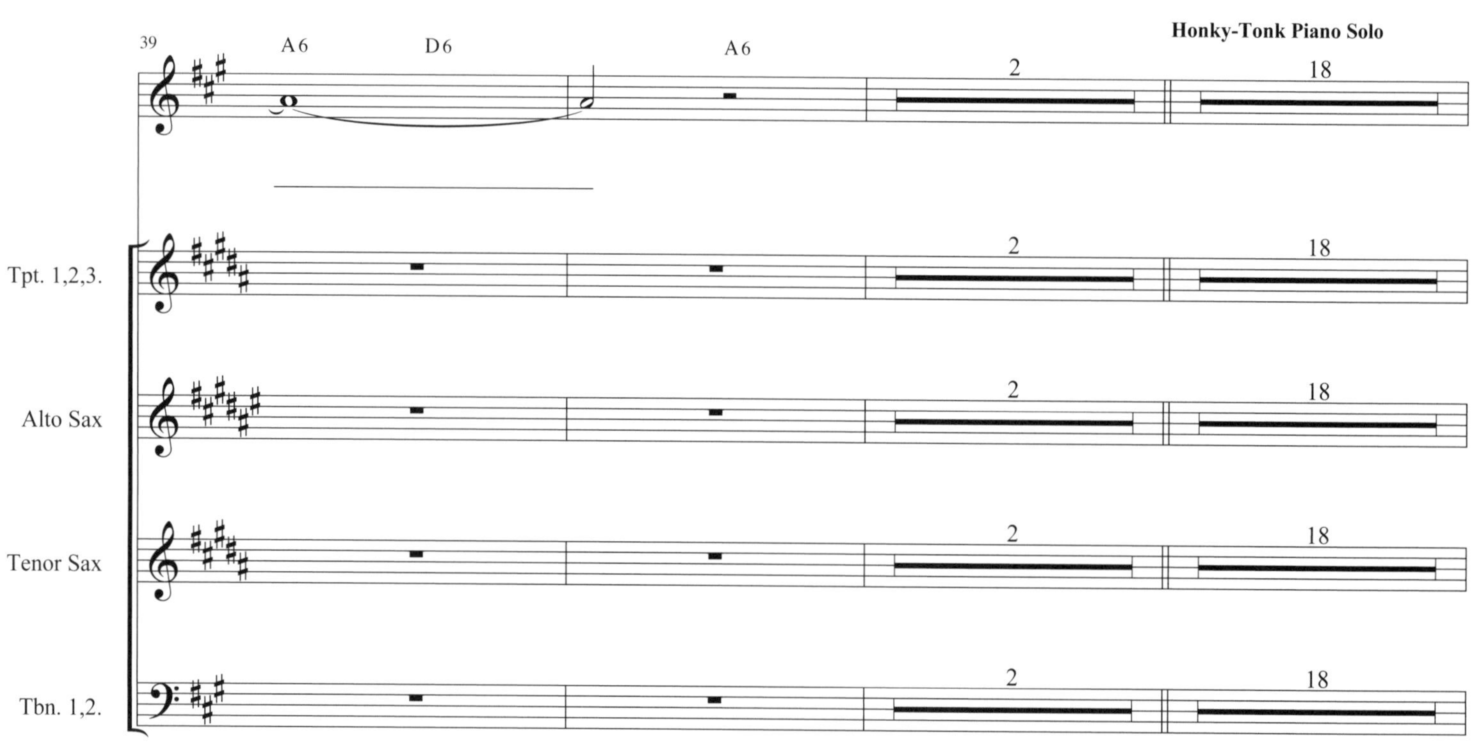
Honky-Tonk Piano Solo
39
A6
D6
A6
2
18
Tpt. 1,2,3.
Alto Sax
Tenor Sax
Tbn. 1,2.

61
A
D
A
D
A
Tpt. 1,2,3.
Alto Sax
Tenor Sax
Tbn. 1,2.

Moderately ♩ = 132
65
A6
D6
A6
D6
A6
D6
A6
D6
2. Now, trou - bles are man - y, they're as
Tpt. 1,2,3.
Alto Sax
Tenor Sax
Tbn. 1,2.

69
A6
D6
A6
D6
A6
D6
A6
D6
deep as a well. I can swear there ain't no heav - en, but I
Tpt. 1,2,3.
Alto Sax
Tenor Sax
Tbn. 1,2.

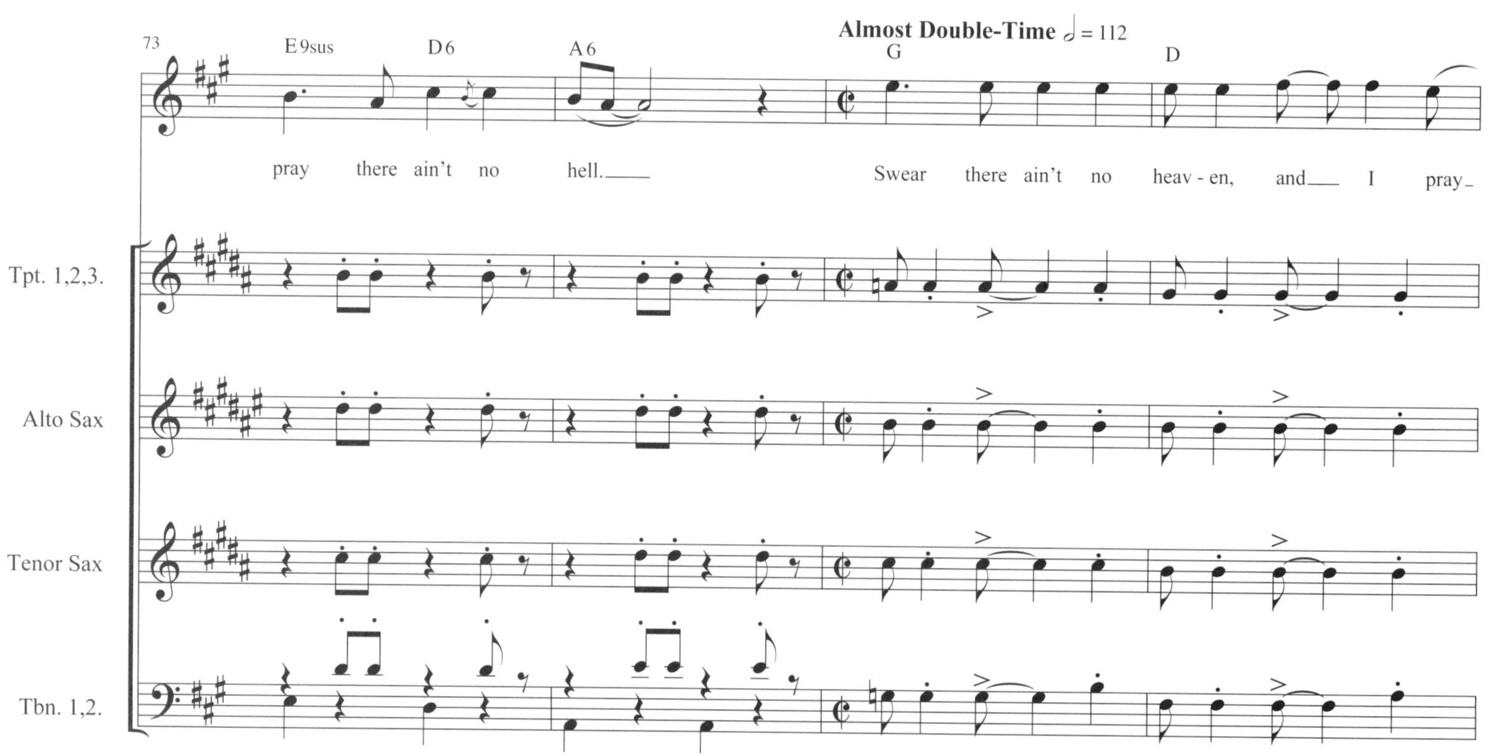
73
E9sus
D6
A6
Almost Double-Time 𝅗𝅥 = 112
G
D
pray there ain't no hell. Swear there ain't no heav - en, and I pray
Tpt. 1,2,3.
Alto Sax
Tenor Sax
Tbn. 1,2.

77
G
D
E7sus
Bm7
C♯m7
D6
E9sus
there ain't no hell, but I'll nev - er know by liv - in', on - ly my
Tpt. 1,2,3.
Alto Sax
Tenor Sax
Tbn. 1,2.

81
A6
D6
A6
D6
A6
D6
A6
dy - in' will tell, yes, on - ly my dy - in' will tell, yeah.
Tpt. 1,2,3.
Alto Sax
Tenor Sax
Tbn. 1,2.

85
D6
C♯m7
B m7
E 9sus
A
D
A
D
On - ly my dy - in' will tell.
And when I
Tpt. 1,2,3.
Alto Sax
Tenor Sax
Tbn. 1,2.

89
B m7
C♯m7
F♯m7
A 7
die, and when I'm gone, there'll be
Tpt. 1,2,3.
Alto Sax
Tenor Sax
Tbn. 1,2.

93
D
C♯m
B m7
E 9sus
one child born in this world to car - ry on, to car - ry
Tpt. 1,2,3.
Alto Sax
Tenor Sax
Tbn. 1,2.

97
A 6
D 6
A 6
D 6
A 6
on, yeah, yeah.
Tpt. 1,2,3.
Alto Sax
Tenor Sax
Tbn. 1,2.
mf
mf

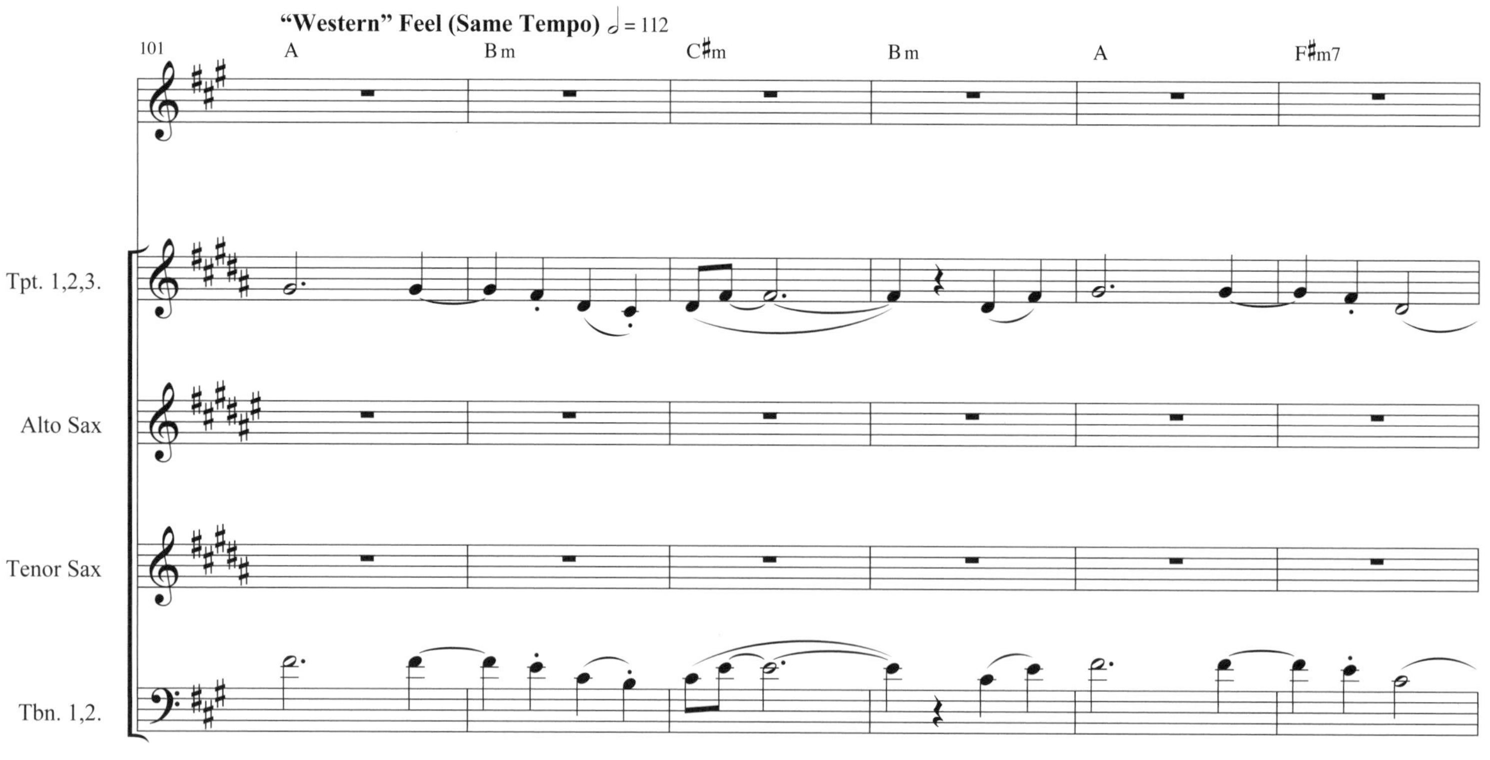
"Western" Feel (Same Tempo) 𝅗𝅥 = 112
101
A
B m
C♯m
B m
A
F♯m7
Tpt. 1,2,3.
Alto Sax
Tenor Sax
Tbn. 1,2.

107
B m7
E7
A
A 7/C♯
D
F
Tpt. 1,2,3.
Alto Sax
Tenor Sax
Tbn. 1,2.

113
B♭
F♯m
Bm
E7
A
D
A
D
A
Tpt. 1,2,3.
Alto Sax
Tenor Sax
Tbn. 1,2.

119
D.S. al Coda
D
A
D
A
Tpt. 1,2,3.
Alto Sax
Tenor Sax
Tbn. 1,2.
f

Coda
Funk (Same Tempo) 𝅗𝅥 = 112
123
A6
D6
A6
A7
go nat-ural - ly. Here I go! Ha! Hey, hey. Here come the
Tpt. 1,2,3.
Alto Sax
Tenor Sax
Tbn. 1,2.

129
dev - il, a right be - hind. Laugh, child - ren! Here he come,
Tpt. 1,2,3.
Alto Sax
Tenor Sax
Tbn. 1,2.
f

135
here he comes,
hey...
Tpt. 1,2,3.
Alto Sax
Tenor Sax
Tbn. 1,2.

141
A
Don't wan-na go by the dev-il,
don't wan-na go by a de-mon,
don't wan-na go by Sa-tan,
Tpt. 1,2,3.
Alto Sax
Tenor Sax
Tbn. 1,2.

Freely
N.C.
147
don't wan - na die un - eas - y. Just let me go natural - ly.
Tpt. 1,2,3.
Alto Sax
Tenor Sax
Tbn. 1,2.

Slow Chorale (Freely)
151
Bm
C♯m
D
E
F
And when I die, and when I'm dead, dead and gone, there'll be
Tpt. 1,2,3.
p
Alto Sax
Tenor Sax
Tbn. 1,2.
p

156
B♭
F♯
D
N.C.
one child born in our world to car - ry on, to car - ry
Tpt. 1,2,3.
Alto Sax
Tenor Sax
Tbn. 1,2.

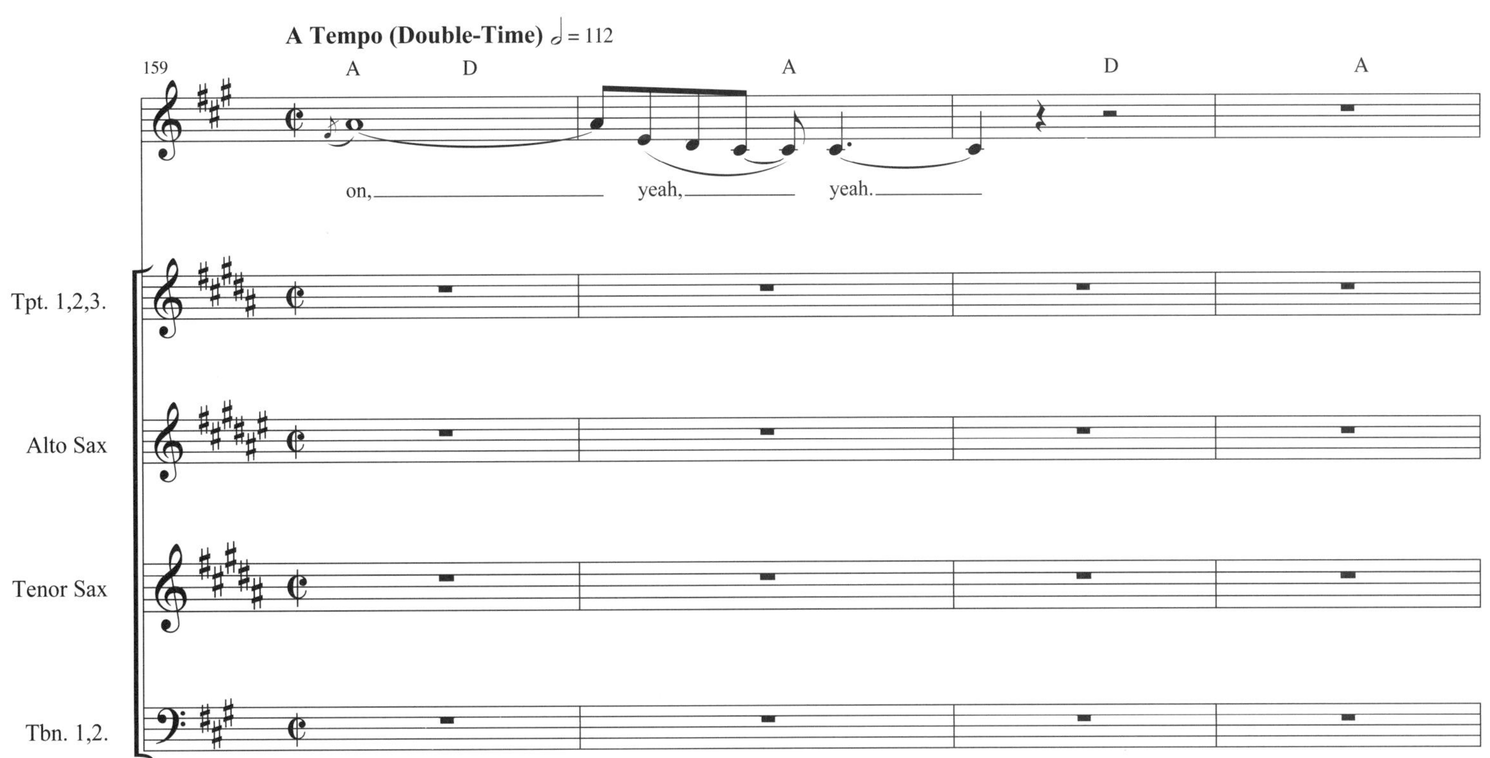
A Tempo (Double-Time) 𝅗𝅥 = 112
159
A
D
A
D
A
on, yeah, yeah.
Tpt. 1,2,3.
Alto Sax
Tenor Sax
Tbn. 1,2.

Additional Lyrics:

Give me my freedom for as long as I be.
All I ask of living is to have no chains on me.
All I ask of living is to have no chains on me,
And all I ask of dying is to go naturally.
Only wanna go naturally.
Here I go! Ha!

To: *Coda*

DOES ANYBODY REALLY KNOW WHAT TIME IT IS?

Words and Music by
ROBERT LAMM

15
E♭maj7♭5
E♭maj7
Shuffle (Same Tempo) ♩= 118
G maj7
C maj7
Solo:
Tpt.
Tenor Sax 1,2.
Tbn. 1,2.
mp
mf
19
G maj7
C maj7
G maj7
C maj7
23
G maj7
C maj7
D
Em
F
Em

27
G
F
B♭maj7
1. As I was walk - ing down the street one day,
2. When I was walk - ing down the street one day,
3. (See additional lyrics)
Tpt.
mp
Tenor Sax 1,2.
mp
Tbn. 1,2.
mp
30
E♭maj7
B♭maj7
E♭maj7
B♭maj7
a man came up to me and asked me what
a pret - ty lad - y looked at me and said
Tpt.
Tenor Sax 1,2.
Tbn. 1,2.
33
E♭maj7
the time was that was on my watch, yeah,
her dia - mond watch had stopped cold dead,
Tpt.
Tenor Sax 1,2.
Tbn. 1,2.

36
D
Em
F
Em
and I
and I
said,
said,
Tpt.
mf
Tenor Sax 1,2.
mf
Tbn. 1,2.
mf
39
Gmaj7
Cmaj7
Gmaj7
"Does an - y - bod - y real - ly know what time it is?
Does an - y - bod - y real - ly
Tpt.
Tenor Sax 1,2.
Tbn. 1,2.
42
Cmaj7
Gmaj7
Cmaj7
Gmaj7
care?
If so, I can't im - ag - ine why
we've all got time
Tpt.
Tenor Sax 1,2.
Tbn. 1,2.

46
1., 2.
Cmaj7
3.
Cmaj7
D
Em
e - nough to cry.
e - nough to die.
Tpt.
Tenor Sax 1,2.
Tbn. 1,2.
49
F
Em
Gmaj7
Cmaj7
Ev - 'ry - bod - y's won - d'rin',
Tpt.
Tenor Sax 1,2.
Tbn. 1,2.
52
Gmaj7
Cmaj7
Gmaj7
and I don't care,
well, a - bout time,
Tpt.
Tenor Sax 1,2.
Tbn. 1,2.

Additional Lyrics:

3. And I was walking down the street one day,
   Being pushed and shoved by people trying to
   Beat the clock, oh, oh, I just don't know,
   I don't know, I don't know.
   And I said, yes I said,
   Chorus

FEELIN' STRONGER EVERY DAY

Words and Music by PETER CETERA
and JAMES PANKOW

15
C
I do be - lieve in you,
Tpt./Flugel
Tenor Sax
Bari. Sax
Tbn. 1,2.

19
E♭
B♭
E♭/B♭
B♭/D
F
and I know you be - lieve in me.
Oh, yeah.
Tpt./Flugel
Tenor Sax
Bari. Sax
Tbn. 1,2.

E♭/B♭ B♭/D F C
22
Oh, yeah. And now we've
Tpt./Flugel
Tenor Sax
Bari. Sax
Tbn. 1,2.

E♭ B♭
26
re - al - ized love's not all that it's s'posed to be.
Tpt./Flugel
Tenor Sax
Bari. Sax
Tbn. 1,2.

E♭/B♭ B♭/D F E♭/B♭ B♭/D F
29
Oh, yeah. Oh, yeah.
Tpt./Flugel
Tenor Sax
Bari. Sax
Tbn. 1,2.

Am7 Dm7
33
And know - ing that you would have want - ed it this way,
Tpt./Flugel
Tenor Sax
Bari. Sax
Tbn. 1,2.

37
Am7
Dm7
F
G
I do be - lieve I'm feel - in' stron - ger ev - 'ry day.
Tpt./Flugel
Tenor Sax
Bari. Sax
Tbn. 1,2.

41
C
I know we real - ly tried, to -
Tpt./Flugel
Tenor Sax
Bari. Sax
Tbn. 1,2.

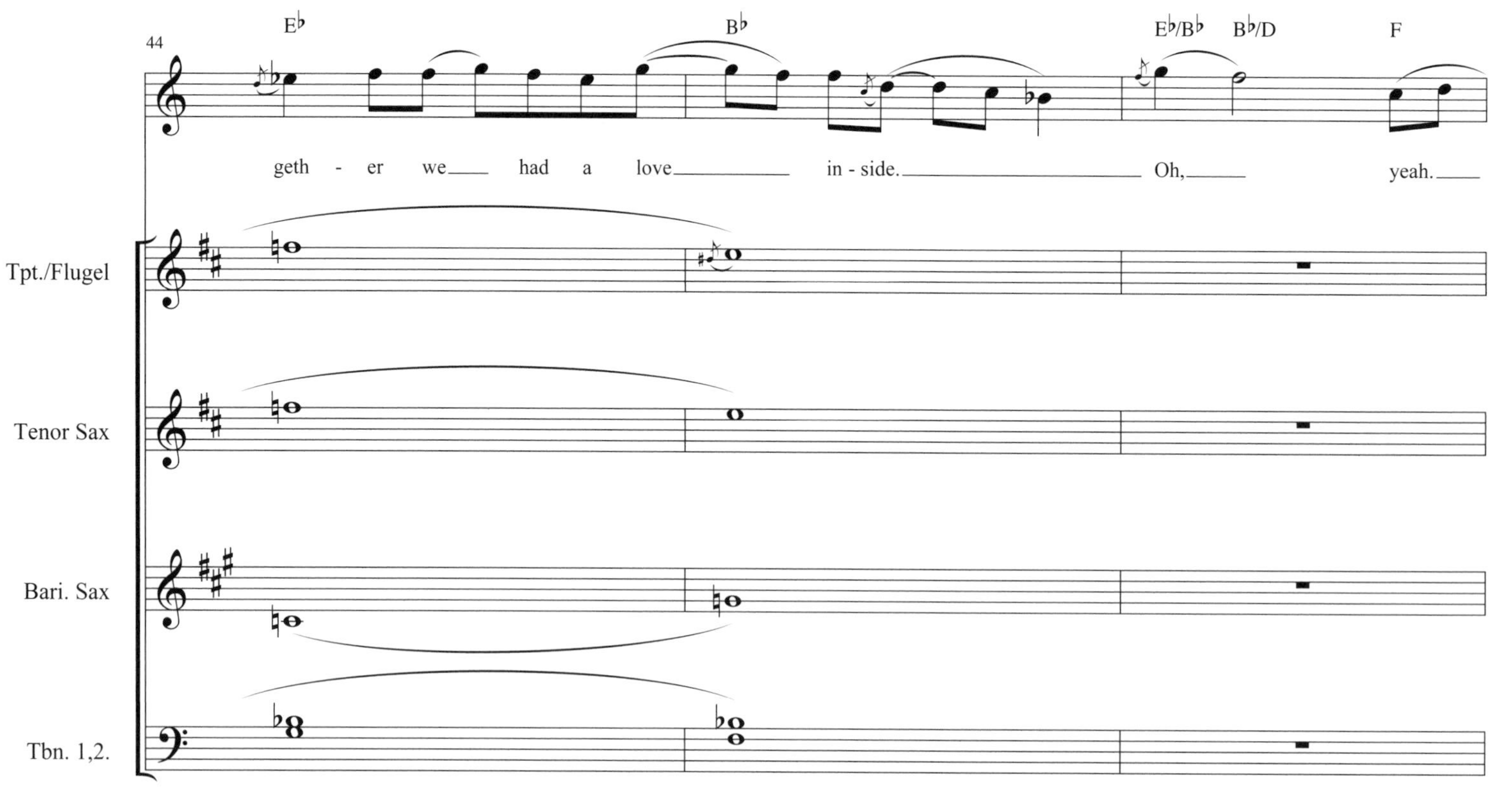
44
E♭
B♭
E♭/B♭
B♭/D
F
geth - er we had a love in - side. Oh, yeah.
Tpt./Flugel
Tenor Sax
Bari. Sax
Tbn. 1,2.

47
E♭/B♭
B♭/D
F
C
Oh, yeah. So now the time has come for
Tpt./Flugel
Tenor Sax
Bari. Sax
Tbn. 1,2.

52
E♭
B♭
E♭/B♭
B♭/D
F
both of us to live on the run.
Oh, yeah.
Tpt./Flugel
Tenor Sax
Bari. Sax
Tbn. 1,2.

56
E♭/B♭
B♭/D
F
A m7
Oh, yeah.
And know - ing that you would have
Tpt./Flugel
Tenor Sax
Bari. Sax
Tbn. 1,2.

60
Dm7
Am7
want - ed it this way,
I do be - lieve I'm feel-in'
Tpt./Flugel
Tenor Sax
Bari. Sax
Tbn. 1,2.

64
Dm7
F
G
stron - ger ev - 'ry day.
Tpt./Flugel
Tenor Sax
Bari. Sax
Tbn. 1,2.

67
C
F
Dm7
G
Yeah,
yeah,
yeah.
Tpt./Flugel
Tenor Sax
Bari. Sax
Tbn. 1,2.

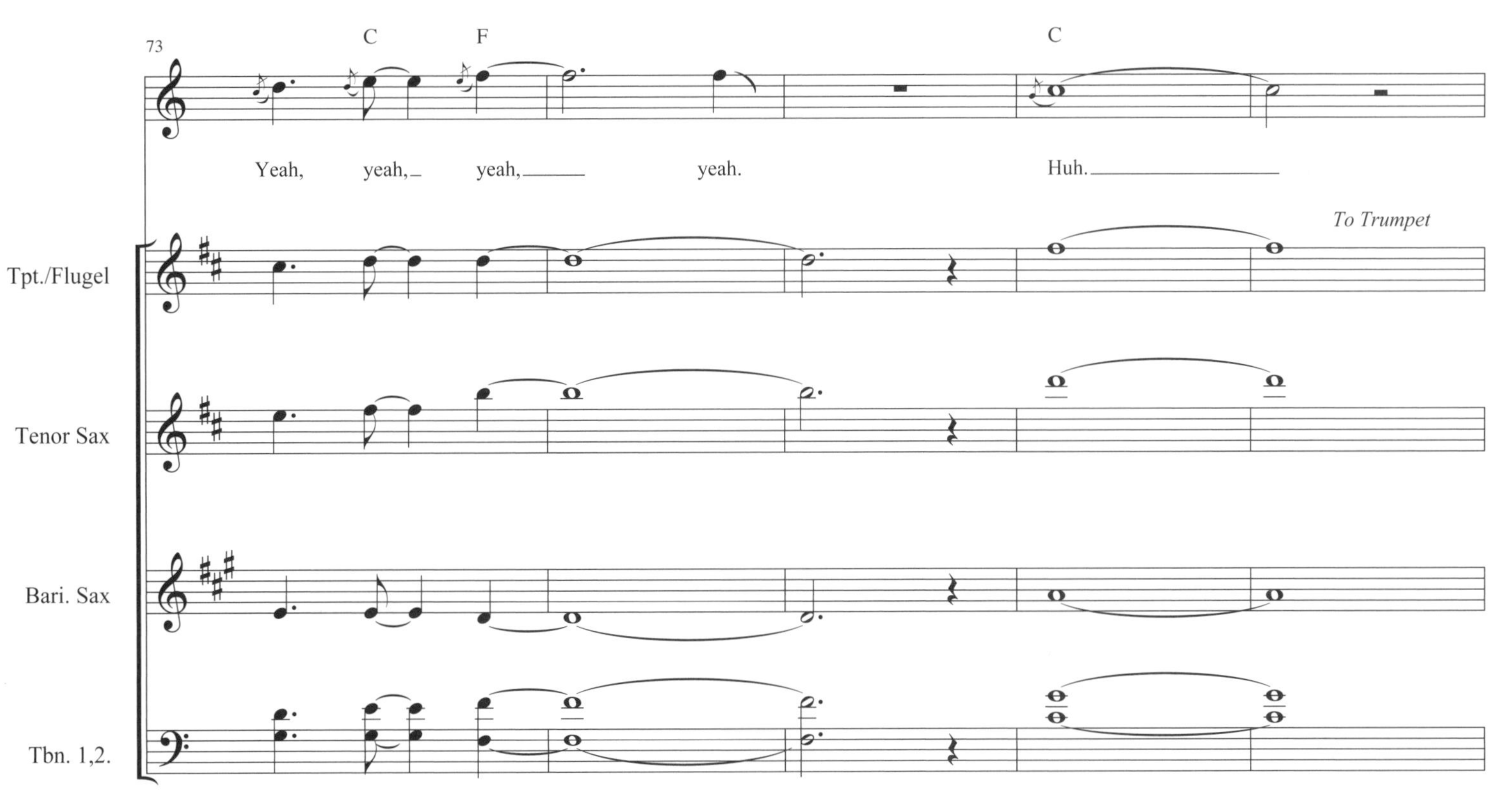
73
C
F
C
Yeah,
yeah,
yeah,
yeah.
Huh.
To Trumpet
Tpt./Flugel
Tenor Sax
Bari. Sax
Tbn. 1,2.

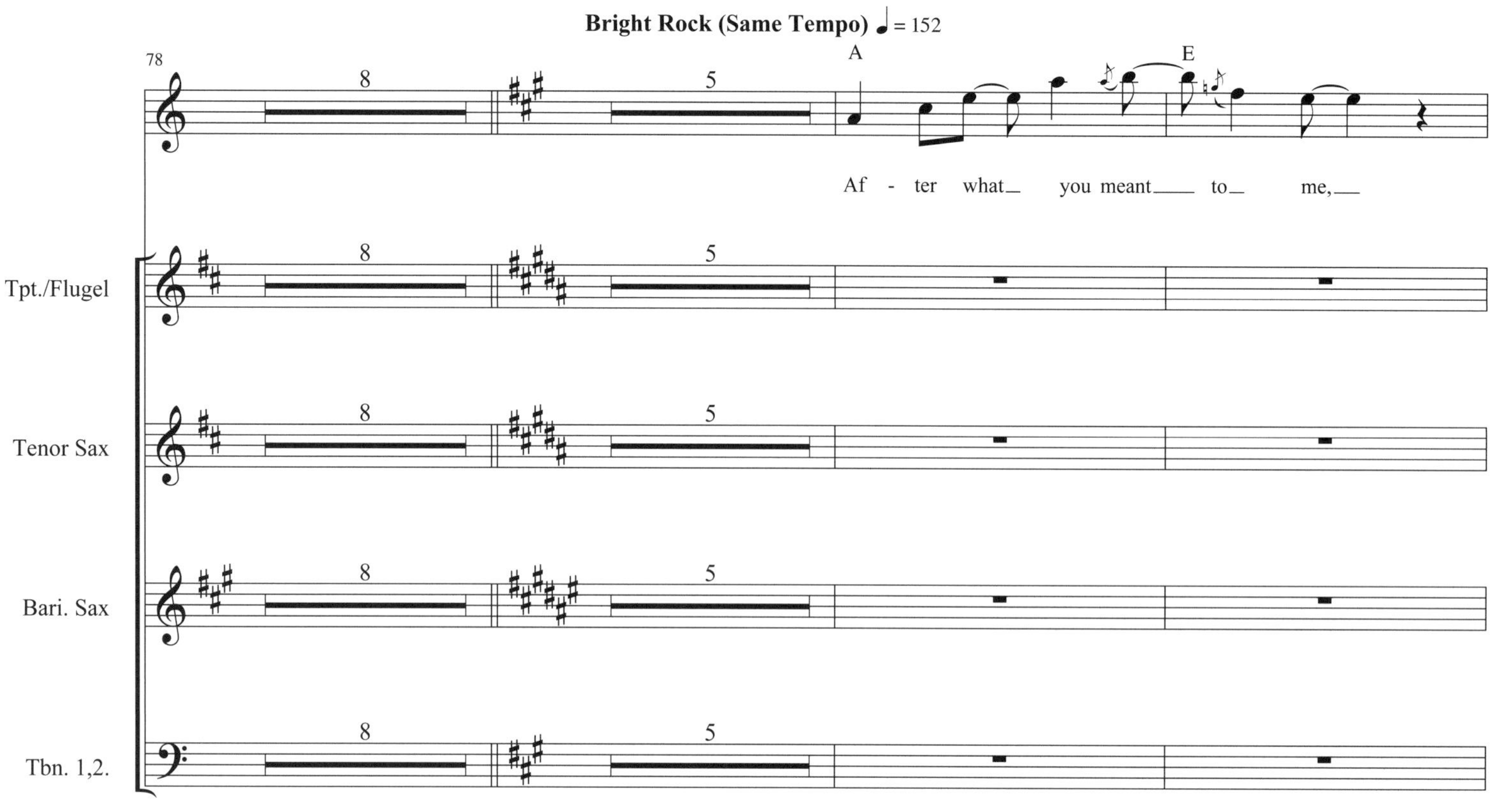
Bright Rock (Same Tempo) ♩ = 152
78
8
5
A
E
Af - ter what you meant to me,
Tpt./Flugel
Tenor Sax
Bari. Sax
Tbn. 1,2.

93
B
F♯
C♯
ooh, ba - by now, I can make it eas - i - ly.
Tpt./Flugel
Tenor Sax
Bari. Sax
Tbn. 1,2.

97
B
A
I know that we both
Trumpet:
Tpt./Flugel
Tenor Sax
Bari. Sax
Tbn. 1,2.

100
E
B
a - gree, the best thing to hap - pen to you, the
Tpt./Flugel
Tenor Sax
Bari. Sax
Tbn. 1,2.

103
F♯
C♯
B
best thing that hap - pen'd to me.
Yeah, yeah,
Tpt./Flugel
Tenor Sax
Bari. Sax
Tbn. 1,2.

106
A
E
B
yeah.
(Vocal tacet 2nd time)
Tpt./Flugel
Tenor Sax
Bari. Sax
Tbn. 1,2.

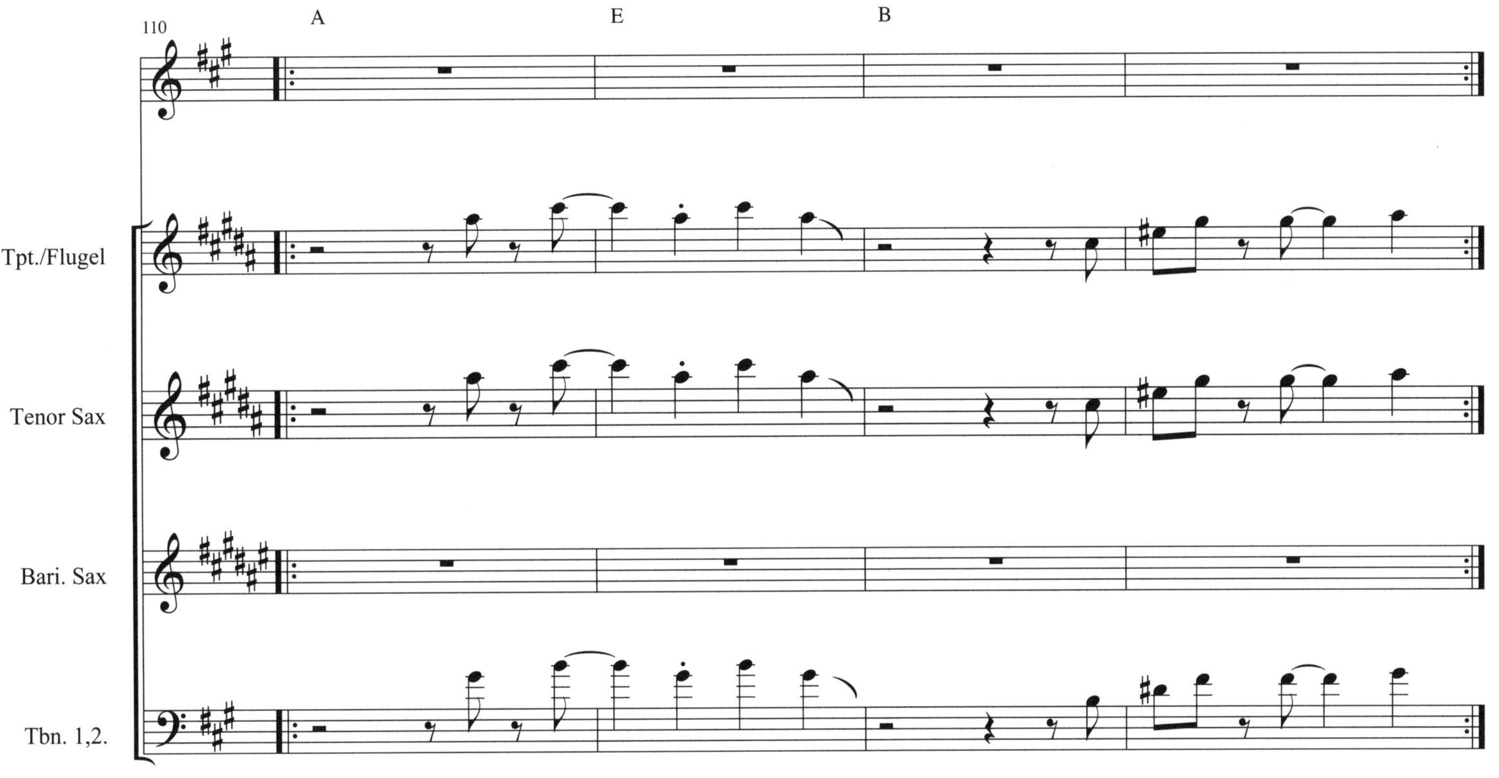
110
A
E
B
Tpt./Flugel
Tenor Sax
Bari. Sax
Tbn. 1,2.

114
A
E
B
Feel - in' stron - ger ev - 'ry day.
Tpt./Flugel
Tenor Sax
Bari. Sax
Tbn. 1,2.

118
A
E
B
Feel - in' stron - ger ev - 'ry day.
Tpt./Flugel
Tenor Sax
Bari. Sax
Tbn. 1,2.

122
A
E
B
Play 10 Times and Fade
Feel - in' stron - ger ev - 'ry day.
Tpt./Flugel
Tenor Sax
Bari. Sax
Tbn. 1,2.

GET IT ON

Words and Music by B. CHASE
and TERRY RICHARD

7
F
1. I need your lov - in', I said I want your lov - in'.
2. (See additional lyrics)
Tpt. 1
Tpt. 2
Tpt. 3
Tpt. 4

11
B♭
I need you ev - 'ry min-ute of the day, now.
C
Girl, lis - ten what I
Tpt. 1
Tpt. 2
Tpt. 3
Tpt. 4

14
N.C.
C
1.
say. Get it on in the morn - in', now.
Tpt. 1
Tpt. 2
Tpt. 3
Tpt. 4
mf
mf
mf
mf

17
2.
F7
I'm gon - na tell you just what I'm gon - na do:
(8va on D.S.)
Tpt. 1
Tpt. 2
Tpt. 3
Tpt. 4
f
f
f
f

20
B♭7
I'm gon-na make love___ to you.
That's___ the kind of feel-in' that just won't quit.
Tpt. 1
Tpt. 2
Tpt. 3
Tpt. 4

23
C7
To Coda
N.C.
I said a-come on, girl, now this is it.___
Get it on in the morn-in', now.
Tpt. 1
Tpt. 2
Tpt. 3
Tpt. 4

26
F
Tpt. 1
Tpt. 2
Tpt. 3
Tpt. 4

29
C
Aw, that feel - in's gon - na be you, a - that feel - in's gon - na be me. It's
Tpt. 1
Tpt. 2
Tpt. 3
Tpt. 4

32
Fmaj7
B♭
gon-na be just you and me in ec-sta-sy.
Tpt. 1
Tpt. 2
Tpt. 3
Tpt. 4

36
Dm7
E♭
A♭
G
C7♯9
Tpt. 1
Tpt. 2
Tpt. 3
Tpt. 4

Organ Solo
41
8
F7♯9
B♭7
Tpt. 1
Tpt. 2
Tpt. 3
Tpt. 4
f

51
F7♯9
B♭7
F7♯9
B♭7
Tpt. 1
Tpt. 2
Tpt. 3
Tpt. 4

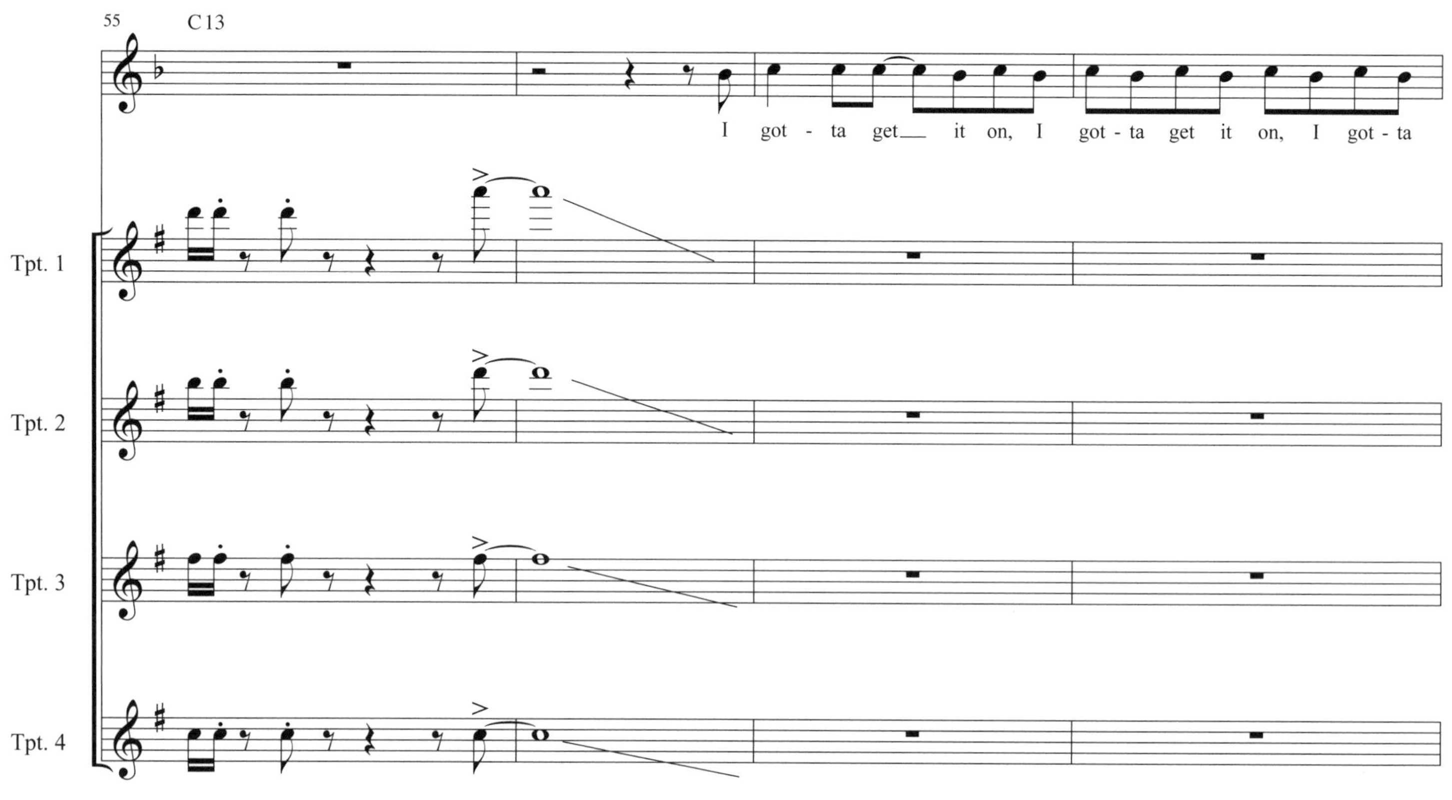
55
C13
I got - ta get___ it on, I got - ta get it on, I got - ta
Tpt. 1
Tpt. 2
Tpt. 3
Tpt. 4

59
D.S. al Coda
get it on,___ I got - ta get it on, I got - ta get it on, I got - ta get it on, I got - ta get it on. I said a
Tpt. 1
Tpt. 2
Tpt. 3
Tpt. 4

Coda
61
C
Aw, that feel - in's gon - na be you, a - that
Tpt. 1
Tpt. 2
Tpt. 3
Tpt. 4
f

64
feel - in's gon - na be me. It's gon - na be just you and me in ec - sta - sy.
Tpt. 1
Tpt. 2
Tpt. 3
Tpt. 4

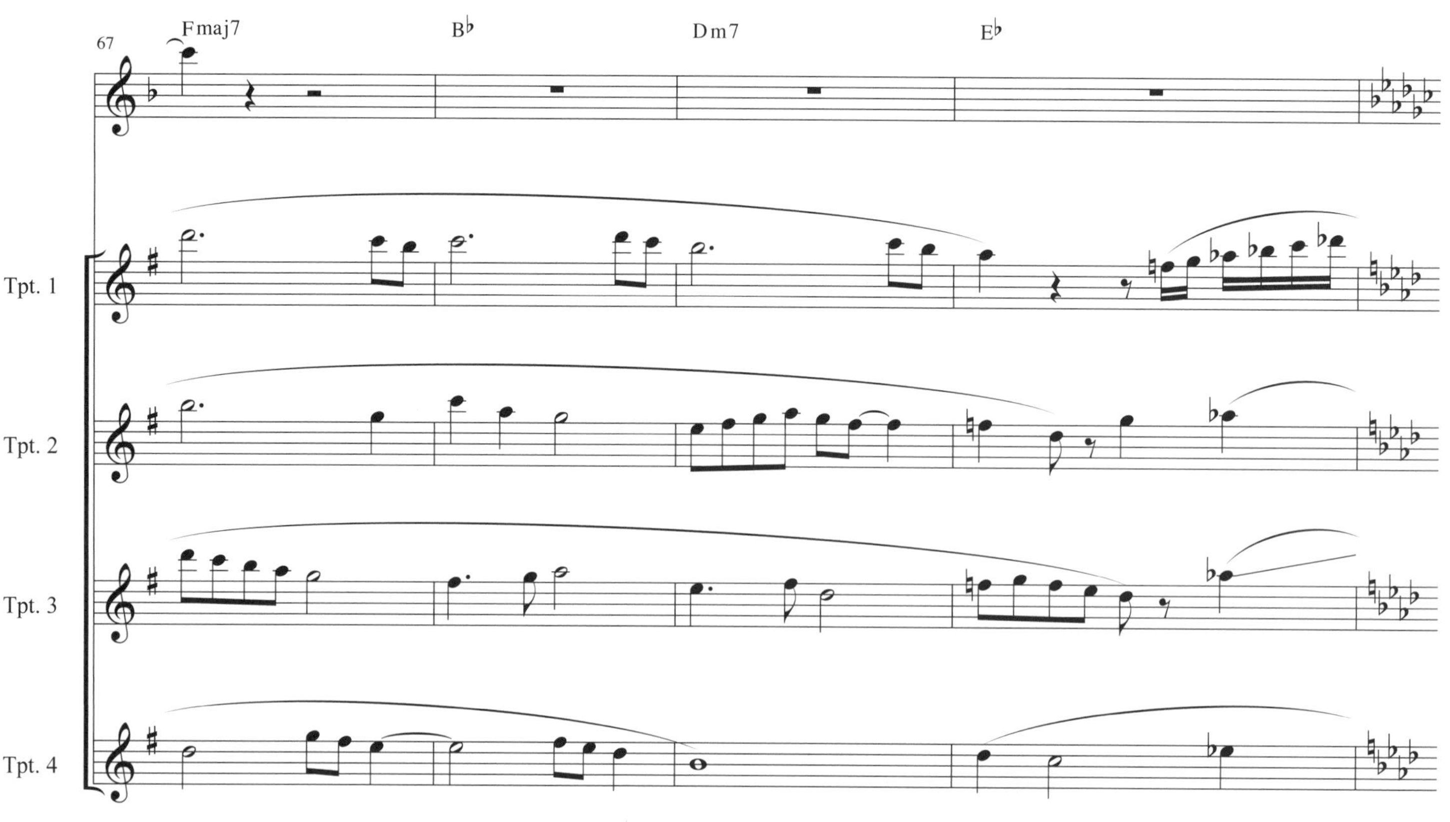
67
Fmaj7
B♭
Dm7
E♭
Tpt. 1
Tpt. 2
Tpt. 3
Tpt. 4

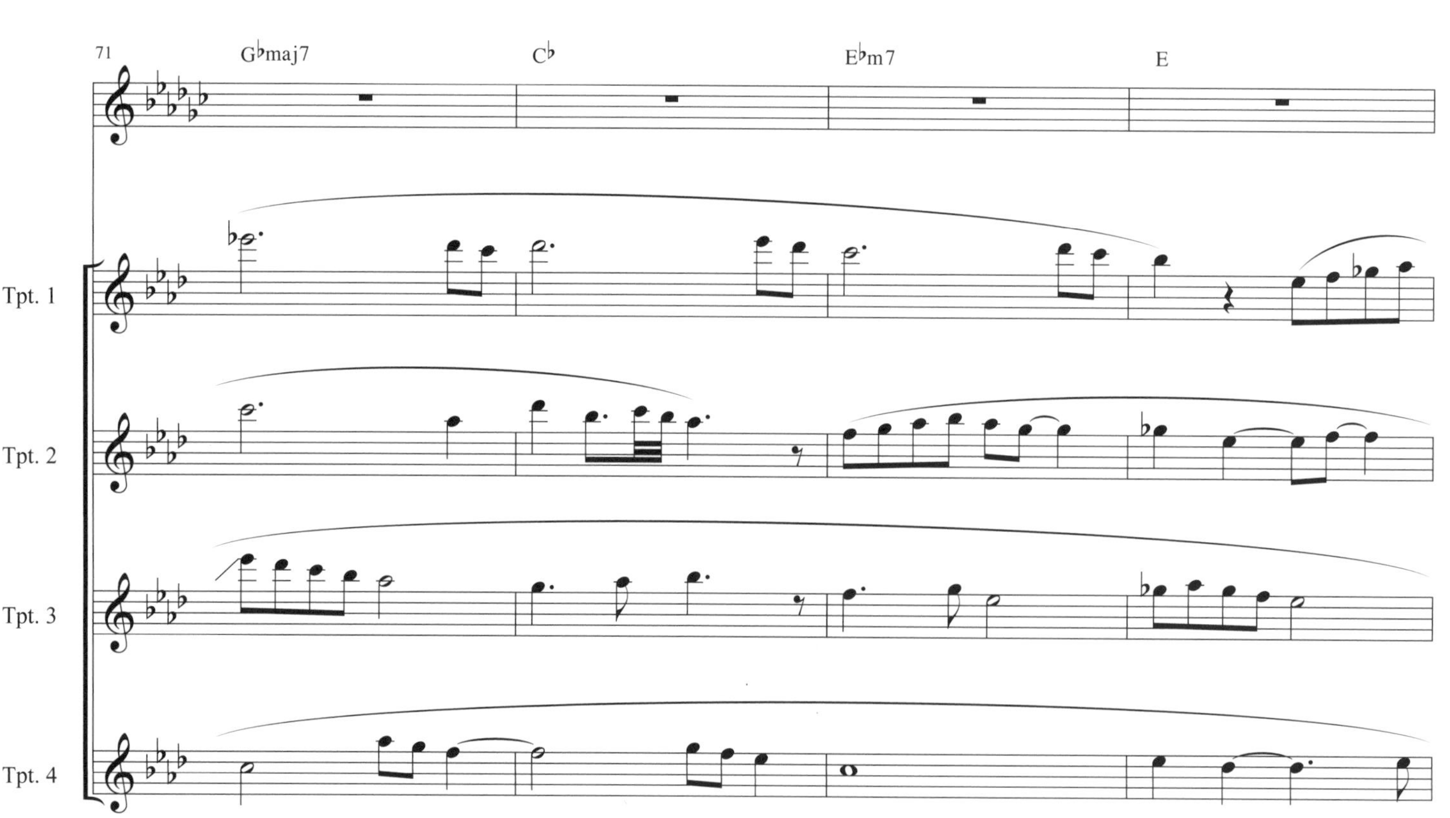
71
G♭maj7
C♭
E♭m7
E
Tpt. 1
Tpt. 2
Tpt. 3
Tpt. 4

Additional Lyrics:

2. I want you when the moon shines bright,
   I said I want you when the time is right, now.
   I need you all through the night, now.
   There are feelings out of sight.
   Get it on in the mornin', now.
   Chorus

HONKY CAT

Words and Music by ELTON JOHN
AND BERNIE TAUPIN

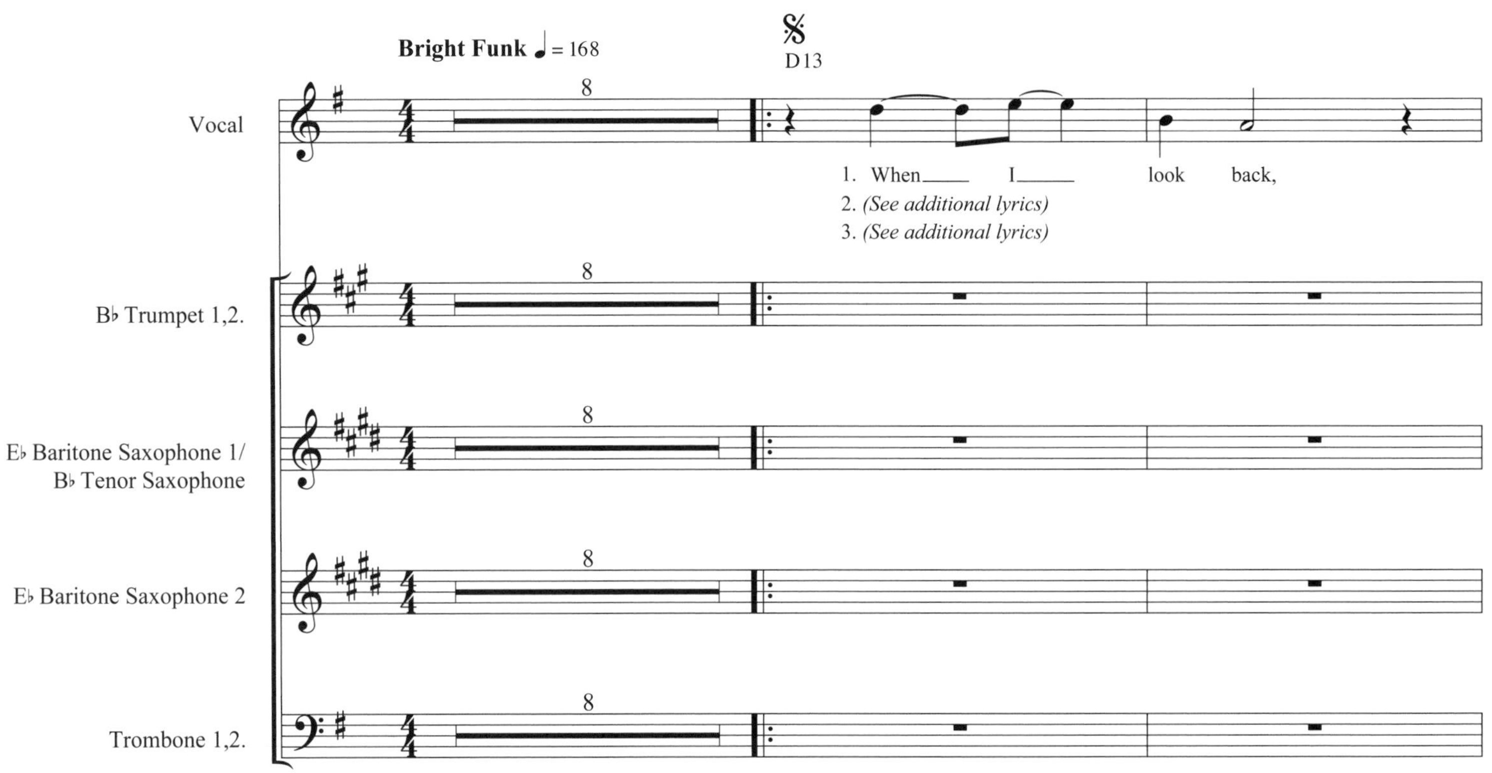

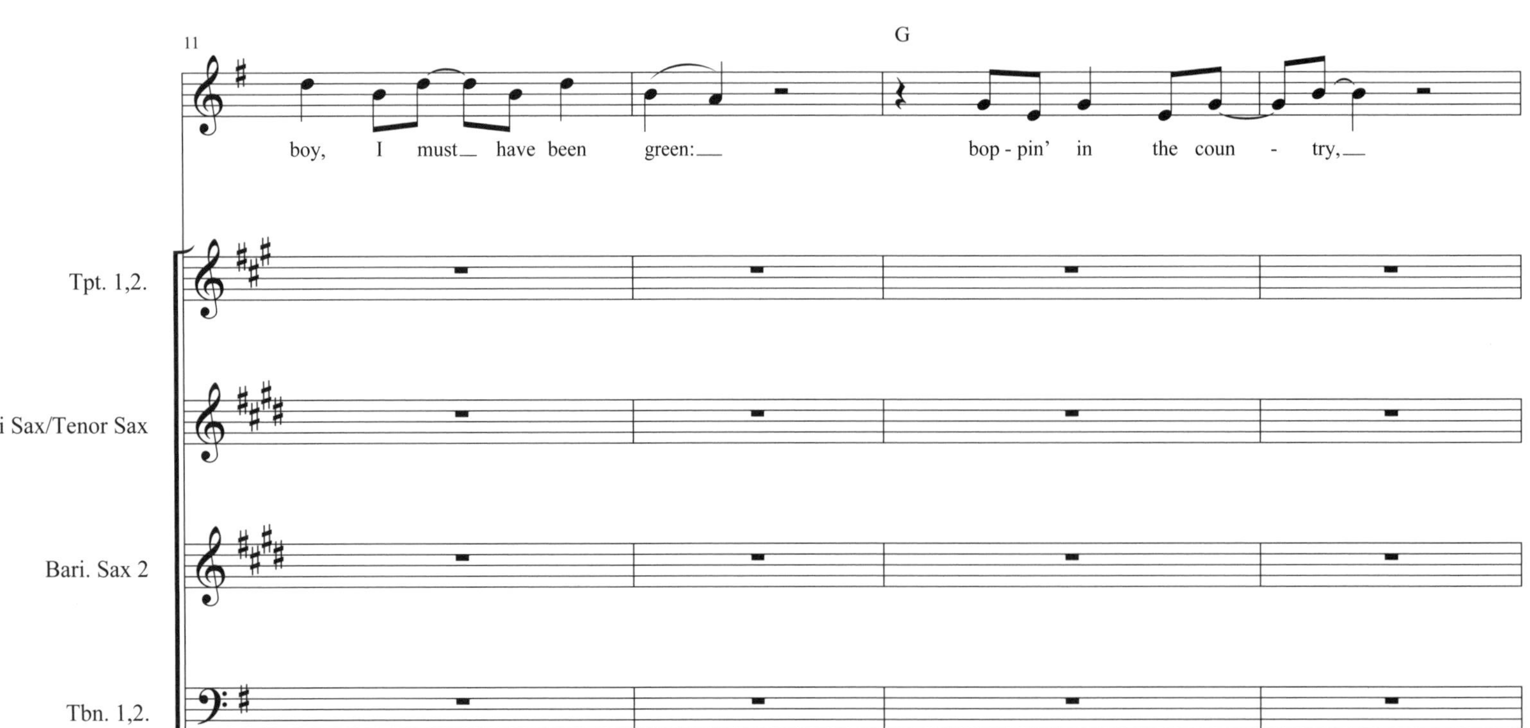

15
D13
fish - in' in a stream,
look - in' for an an - swer,
Tpt. 1,2.
Sax/Tenor Sax
Bari. Sax 2
Tbn. 1,2.

19
G
try - in' to find a sign.
Un - til I saw your cit - y lights,
Tpt. 1,2.
i Sax/Tenor Sax
Bari. Sax 2
Tbn. 1,2.

23
B7
hon - ey, I was blind. They said, "Get back, honk - y cat.
Tpt. 1,2.
Bari Sax
ari Sax/Tenor Sax
Bari. Sax 2
Tbn. 1,2.

27
B7♯5
E7
bet - ter get back to the woods." Well, I quit those days
Tpt. 1,2.
ari Sax/Tenor Sax
Bari. Sax 2
Tbn. 1,2.

30
and my red - neck ways and a,
Tpt. 1,2.
i Sax/Tenor Sax
Bari. Sax 2
Tbn. 1,2.

33
D7
1., 3.
mmm, hmm, hmm, hmm, oh, a change
Tpt. 1,2.
ri Sax/Tenor Sax
Bari. Sax 2
Tbn. 1,2.

36
G
2
— is gon - na do me good.
Tpt. 1,2.
ari Sax/Tenor Sax
Bari. Sax 2
Tbn. 1,2.

40
B 7
"You'd bet - ter get back, honk - y cat, liv - in' in the cit - y ain't
Tpt. 1,2.
ari Sax/Tenor Sax
Bari. Sax 2
Tbn. 1,2.

44
B7♯5
E7
where it's at, it's like try'n' to find gold in a
Tpt. 1,2.
ri Sax/Tenor Sax
Bari. Sax 2
Tbn. 1,2.

47
D7
To Coda
sil - ver mine, it's like try'n' to drink whis - key,
Tpt. 1,2.
ari Sax/Tenor Sax
Bari. Sax 2
Tbn. 1,2.

51
G
2
oh,
from a bot - tle of wine.
Tpt. 1,2.
ri Sax/Tenor Sax
Bari. Sax 2
Tbn. 1,2.

56
2.
G
Well, I
Oh, a change is gon - na do me good.
Tpt. 1,2.
i Sax/Tenor Sax
Bari. Sax 2
Tbn. 1,2.

60
D13
2
Tpt. 1,2.
Sax/Tenor Sax
Bari. Sax 2
Tbn. 1,2.
f

65
G
Tpt. 1,2.
Sax/Tenor Sax
Bari. Sax 2
Tbn. 1,2.
f

70
1.
2.
B7
They said, "Get back, honk-y cat,
Tpt. 1,2.
ari Sax/Tenor Sax
Bari. Sax 2
Tbn. 1,2.

74
B7♯5
E7
bet - ter get back to the woods." Well, I quit those
Tpt. 1,2.
ari Sax/Tenor Sax
Bari. Sax 2
Tbn. 1,2.

77
D7
days and my red - neck ways and a oh, huh,
Tpt. 1,2.
Sax/Tenor Sax
Bari. Sax 2
Tbn. 1,2.

81
huh, huh, oh, a change is gon - na do me good.
Tpt. 1,2.
i Sax/Tenor Sax
Bari. Sax 2
Tbn. 1,2.

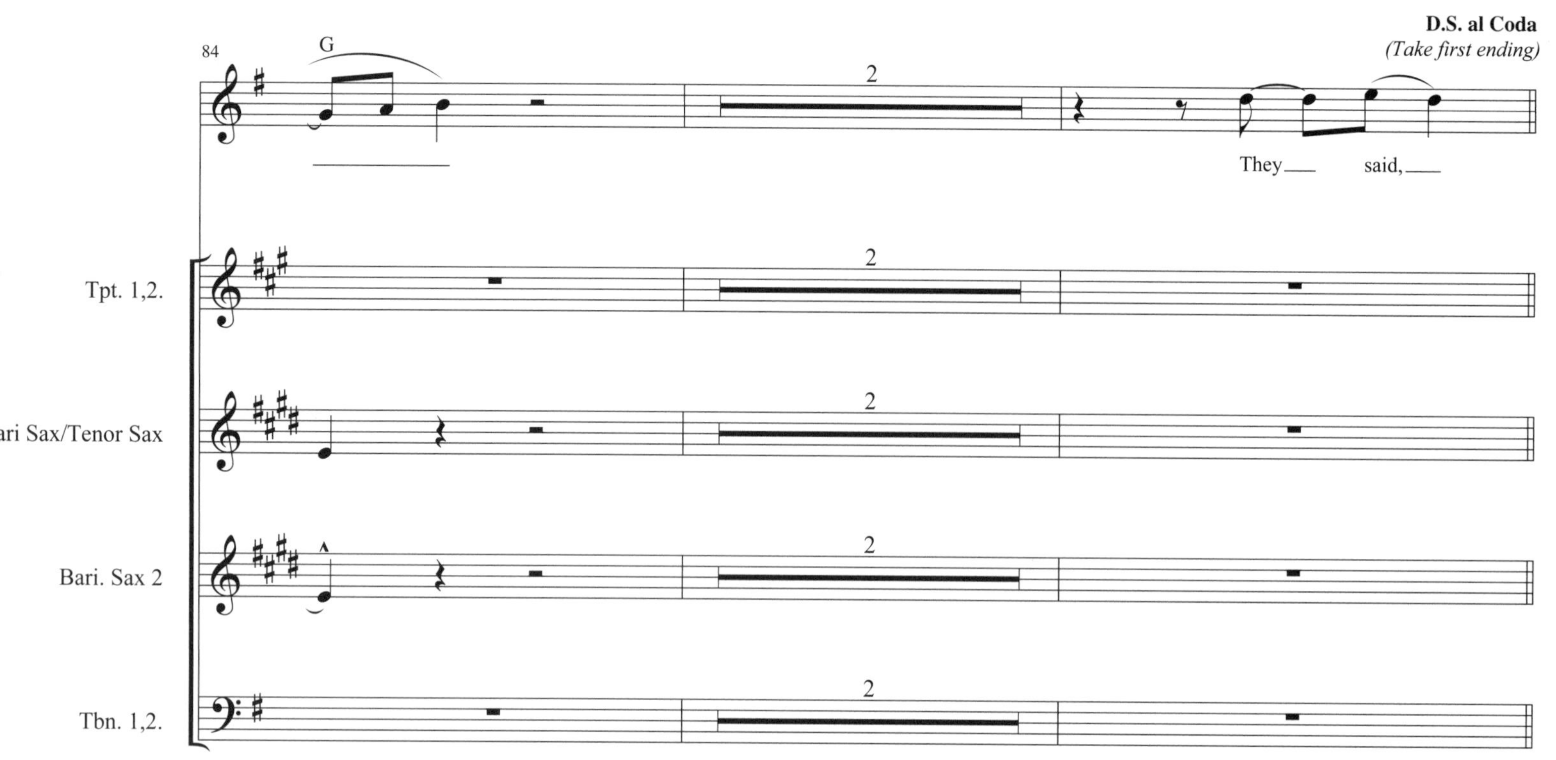
D.S. al Coda
(Take first ending)
84
G
2
They said,
Tpt. 1,2.
Bari Sax/Tenor Sax
Bari. Sax 2
Tbn. 1,2.

Coda
88
G
oh, from a bot - tle of wine.
Tpt. 1,2.
Bari Sax/Tenor Sax
To Tenor
Bari. Sax 2
Tbn. 1,2.

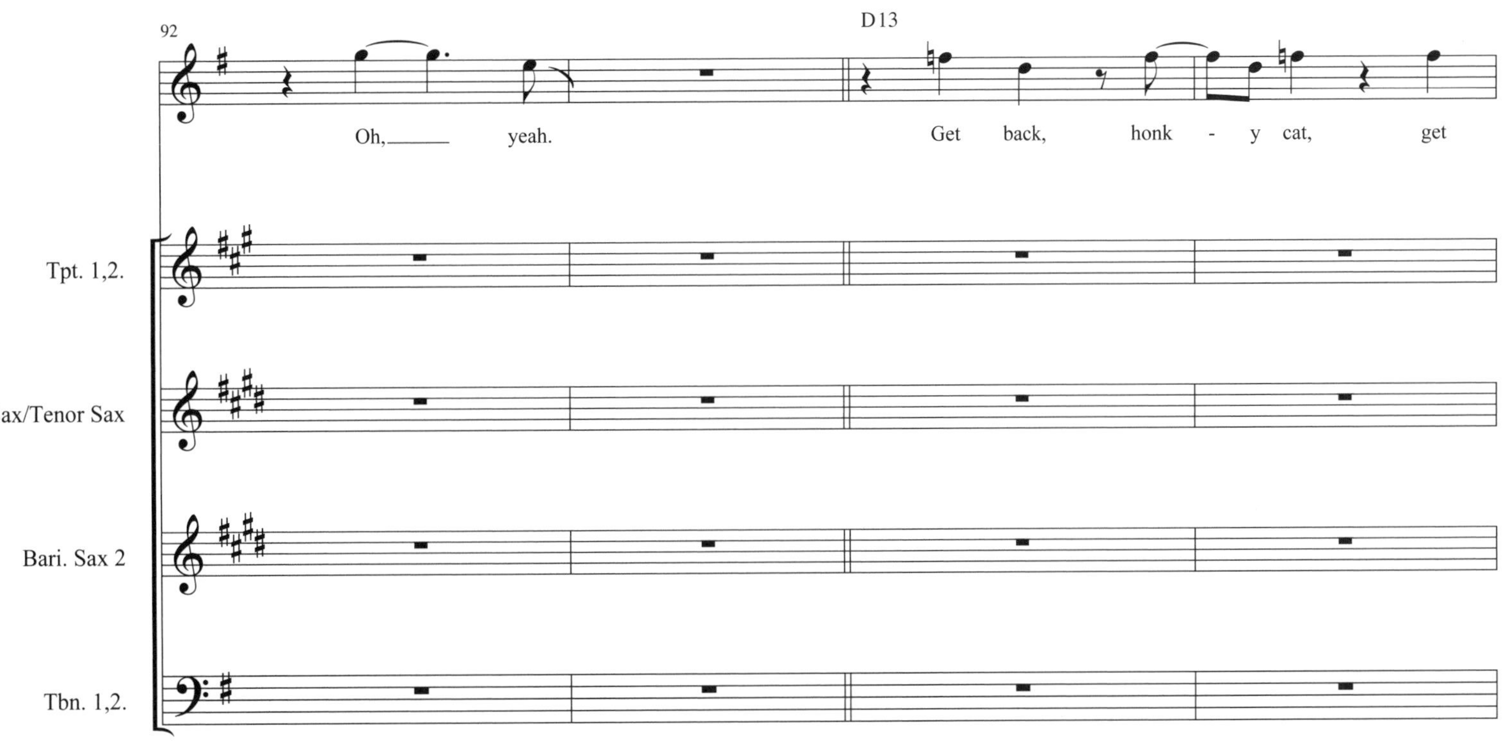
92
D13
Oh, yeah.
Get back, honk - y cat, get
Tpt. 1,2.
Sax/Tenor Sax
Bari. Sax 2
Tbn. 1,2.

96
G
back, honk - y cat, get back.
Hoo!
Tpt. 1,2.
Tenor Sax
i Sax/Tenor Sax
Bari. Sax 2
Tbn. 1,2.
f

100
D13
Get back, honk -
Tpt. 1,2.
T. Sx.
Bari. Sax 2
Tbn. 1,2.

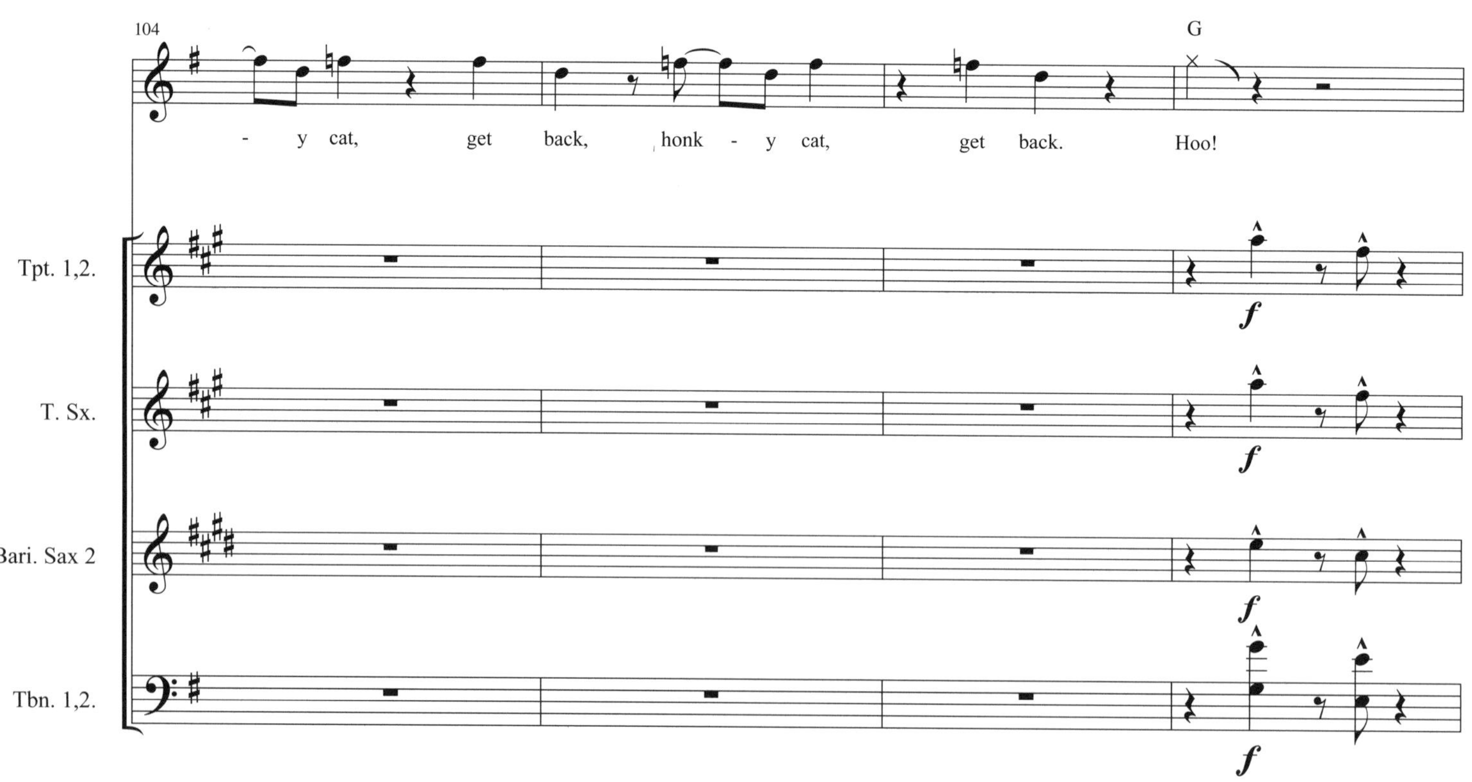
104
G
- y cat, get back, honk - y cat, get back. Hoo!
Tpt. 1,2.
T. Sx.
Bari. Sax 2
Tbn. 1,2.
f

108
D13
Tpt. 1,2.
T. Sx.
Bari. Sax 2
Tbn. 1,2.

112
3
G
Tpt. 1,2.
T. Sx.
Bari. Sax 2
Tbn. 1,2.
f

118
D13
Tpt. 1,2.
T. Sx.
Bari. Sax 2
Tbn. 1,2.
3
3
3
3
3

123
G
Tpt. 1,2.
T. Sx.
Bari. Sax 2
Tbn. 1,2.
f
f
f

126
D13
Get back, honk - y cat, get
(Lead vocal ad lib. 2nd time)
Tpt. 1,2.
T. Sx.
Bari. Sax 2
Tbn. 1,2.

129
G
back, get back, honk' cat, whoo!
Tpt. 1,2.
T. Sx.
Bari. Sax 2
Tbn. 1,2.
f
f
f
f

Additional Lyrics:

2. Well I read some books and I read some magazines
About those high class ladies down in New Orleans,
And all the folks back home well, said I was a fool
They said, "Oh, believe in the Lord is the golden rule."
Chorus

3. They said, "Stay at home boy, you gotta tend the farm.
Living in the city boy, is going to break your heart."
But how can you stay, when your heart says no?
How can you stop when your feet say go?
Chorus

THE HORSE

Music by JESSE JAMES

* *Chord symbols in this song are concert pitched.*

22
B♭
Gm
B♭
Gm
Tpt. 1,2
Tenor Sax
Tbn.
Bari. Sax
26
B♭
Gm
B♭
1.
Gm
2.
Gm
Tpt. 1,2
Tenor Sax
Tbn.
Bari. Sax
31
Dm7
Cm7
Gm
To Coda
Tpt. 1,2
Tenor Sax
Tbn.
Bari. Sax

35
Tpt. 1,2
Tenor Sax
Tbn.
Bari. Sax
8
Dm7
Cm7
Dm7
Cm7
47
Dm7
Cm7
Gm
D.S. al Coda
Coda
51
B♭
Gm
B♭
Gm
Repeat and Fade

THE LETTER

Words and Music by
WAYNE CARSON THOMPSON

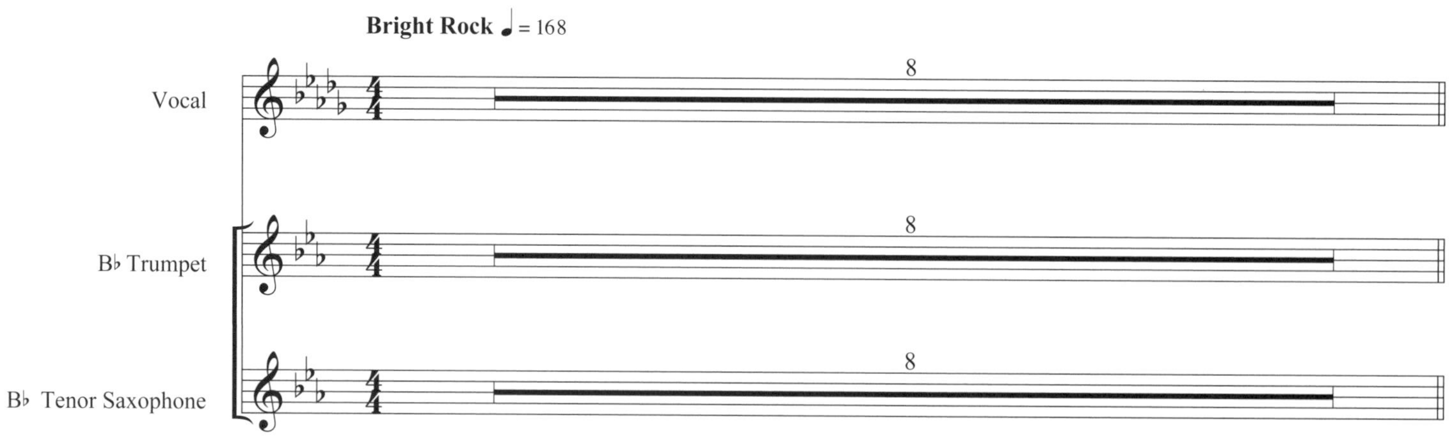

17
B♭m
B♭m/A♭
Gm7♭5
G♭
Oh, the lone - ly days are gone, I'm com - in' home.
Tpt.
Tenor Sax
21
F7
B♭m D♭ E♭ D♭ E♭ D♭
Well, my ba - by, she wrote me a let - ter.
f
25
B♭m D♭ E♭ D♭ E♭ D♭
B♭m7
I don't care how much I've got
29
G♭7
B♭m7
to spend,
I'm gon' find my way,
mp

33
E♭7
B♭m
B♭m/A♭
my way back home a - gain. Oh, the lone - ly days are gone.
Tpt.
Tenor Sax
37
Gm7♭5
G♭
F7
I'm com - in' home. Yeah, my ba - by, she wrote me a let -
41
B♭m D♭ E♭ D♭ E♭ D♭
- ter. Well, she
45
D♭
A♭
G♭
D♭
wrote me the let - ter, said that she could - n't live with - out

49
A♭
me no more.
Tpt.
Tenor Sax
53
D♭
A♭
G♭
D♭
Lis - ten to me, mis - ter, lis - ten to me rav - in' for my
Tpt.
Tenor Sax
57
A♭
F7
ba - by once more.
An - y - way, yeah.
Tpt.
Tenor Sax
61
B♭m7
G♭7
I don't care how much I've got to spend,
Play on D.S. only
Tpt.
mp
Play on D.S. only
Tenor Sax
mp

65
B♭m7
E♭7
I'm gon' find my way, I'm gon' find my way back home a-gain.
Tpt.
Tenor Sax
69
B♭m
B♭m/A♭
Gm7♭5
G♭
Oh, the lone - ly days are gone. I'm com - in' home, yes, sir.
Tpt.
Tenor Sax
73
F7
B♭m
D♭
Well, my ba - by, she wrote me a let - ter.
Tpt.
Tenor Sax
To Coda
76
E♭
D♭
E♭
D♭
B♭m
D♭
E♭
D♭
E♭
D♭
Tpt.
Tenor Sax

1st time: Trumpet solo
2nd time: Tenor solo
1.
2.
E♭ D♭ E♭ D♭
D.S. al Coda
Well, she
Tpt.
Tenor Sax
Coda
Play 8 times
(Lead vocal ad lib.)
B♭m D♭
E♭ D♭ E♭ D♭
B♭m D♭
E♭ D♭ E♭ D♭
B♭m D♭
Tpt.
Tenor Sax
E♭ D♭ E♭ D♭
B♭m
C/B♭
Tpt.
Tenor Sax

LOVE IS ON THE WAY

Words and Music by
JAMES M. PETERIK

17
Tpt. Solo
Tpt. 1,2.
Tpt. 3,4.
f
21
(Flutter)
25
Dm9

29
N. C.
4
A m7
This was the year when the dreams
Tpt. Solo
Tpt. 1,2.
Tpt. 3,4.
36
of man were fi - nal - ly laid un - to rest,
but you know they say that hope
40
springs e - ter - nal with - in the hum - an breast.
Yeah.

43
D m7
G/D
D m7
Some peo - ple die and some peo - ple con - quer, but a change has got to
(Lead vocal ad lib. on D.S.)
Tpt. Solo
Tpt. 1,2.
mf
Tpt. 3,4.
mf
46
E7/G♯
E7
F maj7
come. Love is on the way, hey, hey,
Tpt. Solo
Tpt. 1,2.
f
Tpt. 3,4.
f
49
C maj7
A m7
E m7
hey, hey, hey, hey. Love is on the
Tpt. Solo
Tpt. 1,2.
Tpt. 3,4.

52
F maj7
C maj7
A m7
way, hey, hey, hey, hey, hey, hey.
Tpt. Solo
Tpt. 1,2.
Tpt. 3,4.
To Coda
55
E m7
A m7
B m7
C 6
D
Love is gon' a long, it's gon' a long, it's gon-na take
58
E7sus
A m7
time.
ff
mp

62
Am7
This is the year when we'll find a path and
Tpt. Solo
Tpt. 1,2.
Tpt. 3,4.
mf
mf
66
take it to the rain - bow's end. And there will be no ly -
Tpt. Solo
Tpt. 1,2.
f
Tpt. 3,4.
69
D. S. al Coda
- in', since the truth ain't meant to bend. Yeah.
Tpt. Solo
Tpt. 1,2.
mf
f
Tpt. 3,4.
f

Coda
72
Dm7
G/D
Dm7
E7/G♯
time.
(Lead vocal ad lib.)
Tpt. Solo
Tpt. 1,2.
Tpt. 3,4.
76
E7
Fmaj7
Cmaj7
Love is on the way, hey, hey, hey, hey,
79
Am7
Em7
Fmaj7
hey, hey. Love is on the way, hey, hey,

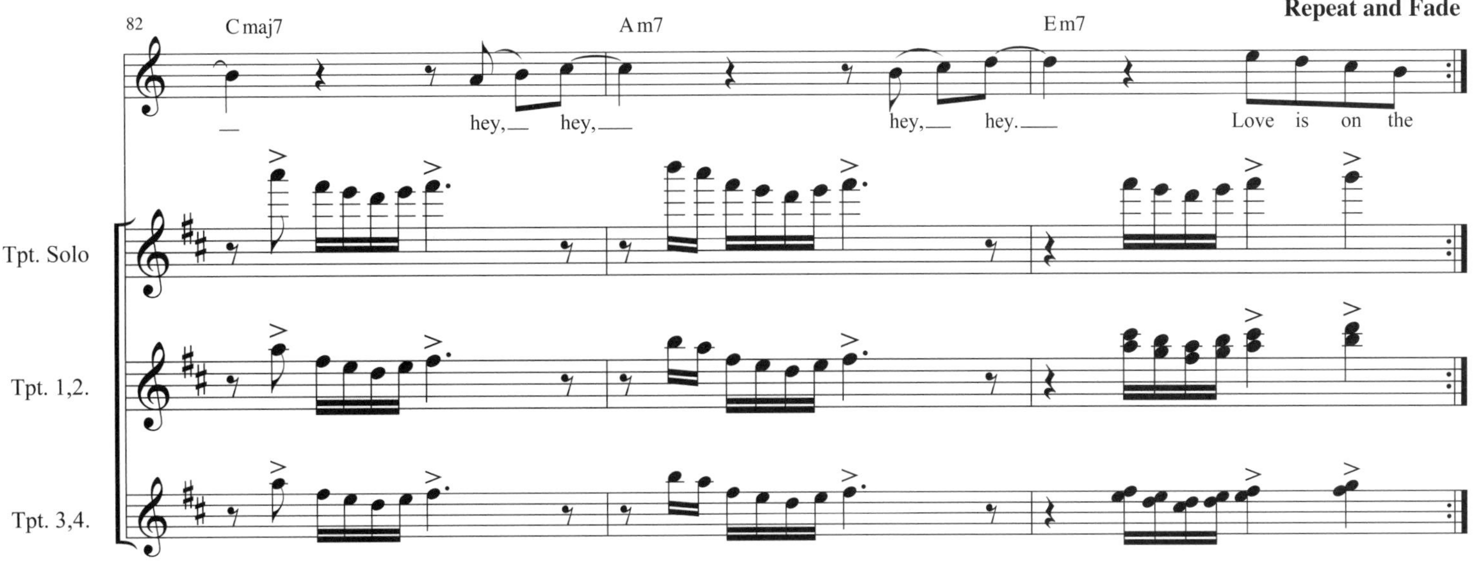
82
Cmaj7
Am7
Em7
Repeat and Fade
hey, hey,
hey, hey.
Love is on the
Tpt. Solo
Tpt. 1,2.
Tpt. 3,4.

MAKE ME SMILE

Words and Music by
JAMES PANKOW

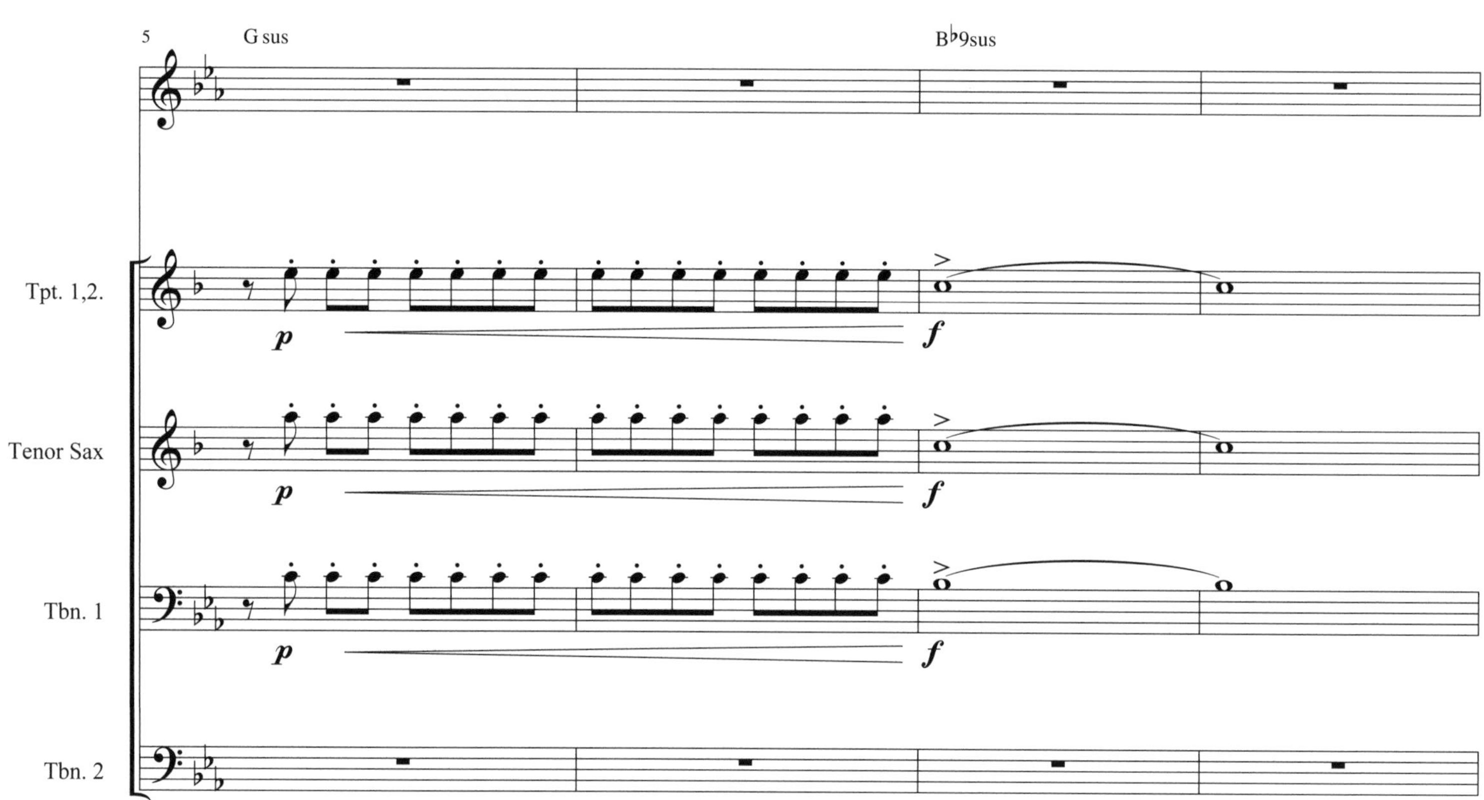

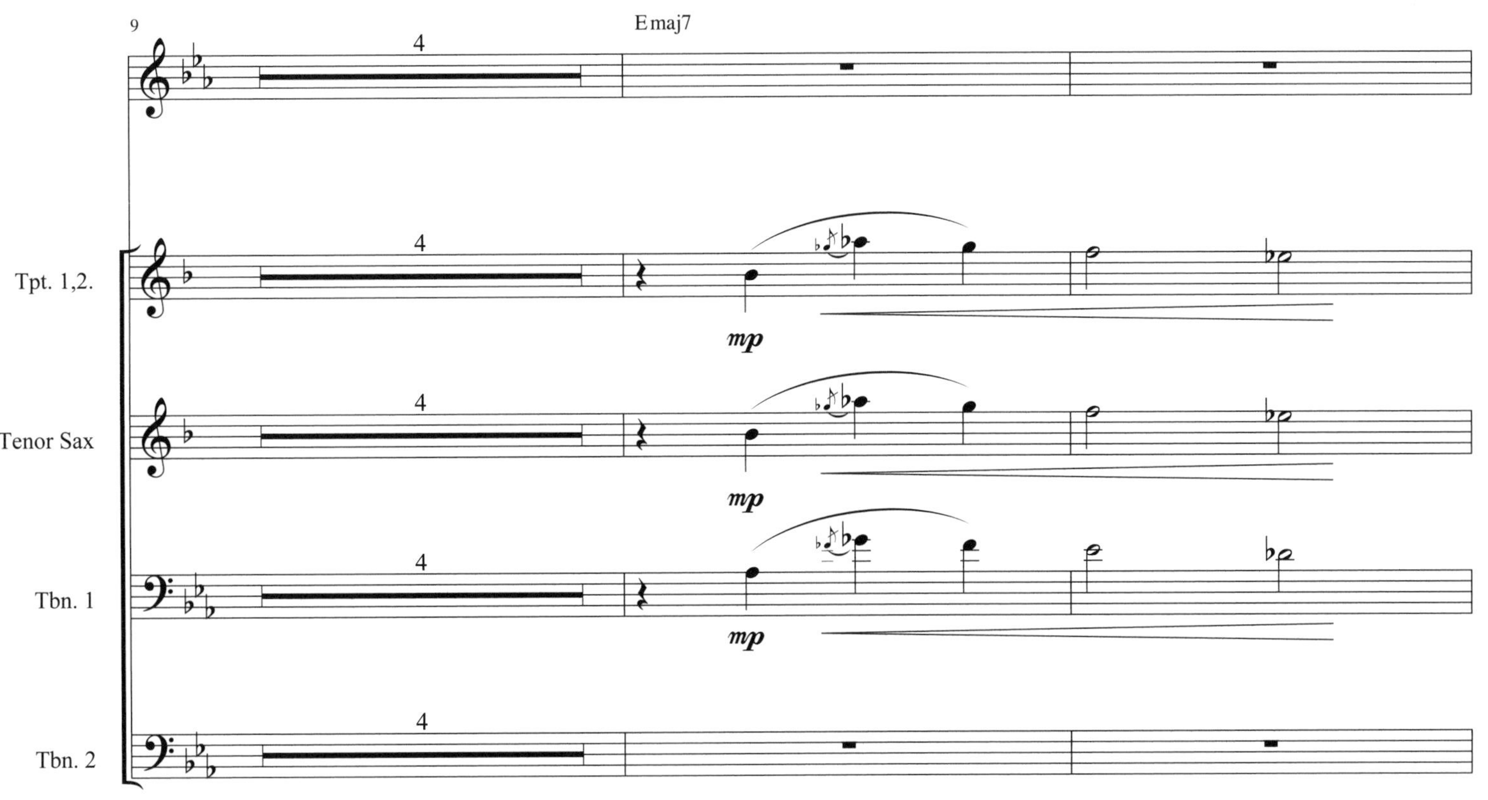
9
Emaj7
4
Tpt. 1,2.
Tenor Sax
Tbn. 1
Tbn. 2
mp

15
Gmaj7
A♭sus
Tpt. 1,2.
Tenor Sax
Tbn. 1
Tbn. 2
f

19
Cm
A♭
E♭
Dm7
G7
3
Child-ren play in the park. They don't know
Tpt. 1,2.
Tenor Sax
Tbn. 1
Tbn. 2

23
Cm
A♭
E♭
Dm7
G7
I'm a - lone in the dark, e - ven though
Tpt. 1,2.
Tenor Sax
Tbn. 1
Tbn. 2

27
Cm
B♭/D
E♭
Fm7
G sus
G
time and time a - gain I see your face smil - in' in - side.
Tpt. 1,2.
Tenor Sax
Tbn. 1
Tbn. 2

31
E♭
D♭
A♭
E♭
D♭
A♭
I'm so hap - py that you love me.
(Lead vocal ad lib.)
Tpt. 1,2.
mf
Tenor Sax
mf
Tbn. 1
mf
Tbn. 2

35
E♭
D♭
A♭
E♭
D♭
A♭
Life is love - ly
when you're near me.
Tpt. 1,2.
Tenor Sax
Tbn. 1
Tbn. 2

39
E♭
E♭/D
Cm
E♭
B♭
To Coda
A♭sus
Tell me you will stay,
make me smile.
Tpt. 1,2.
Tenor Sax
Tbn. 1
Tbn. 2
f
pp
mf

43
Cm
A♭
E♭
Dm7
G7
3
Liv - in' life _ is ___ just _ a game, _ so they say. ____
Tpt. 1,2.
Tenor Sax
Tbn. 1
Tbn. 2

47
Cm
A♭
E♭
Dm7
G7
3
All the games ___ we used to play ___ fade a - way. ______
Tpt. 1,2.
Tenor Sax
Tbn. 1
Tbn. 2

D.S. al Coda
51
Cm
B♭/D
E♭
Fm7
Gsus
G
We may now en - joy the dreams we've shared so long a - go.
Tpt. 1,2.
Tenor Sax
Tbn. 1
Tbn. 2
p
mf

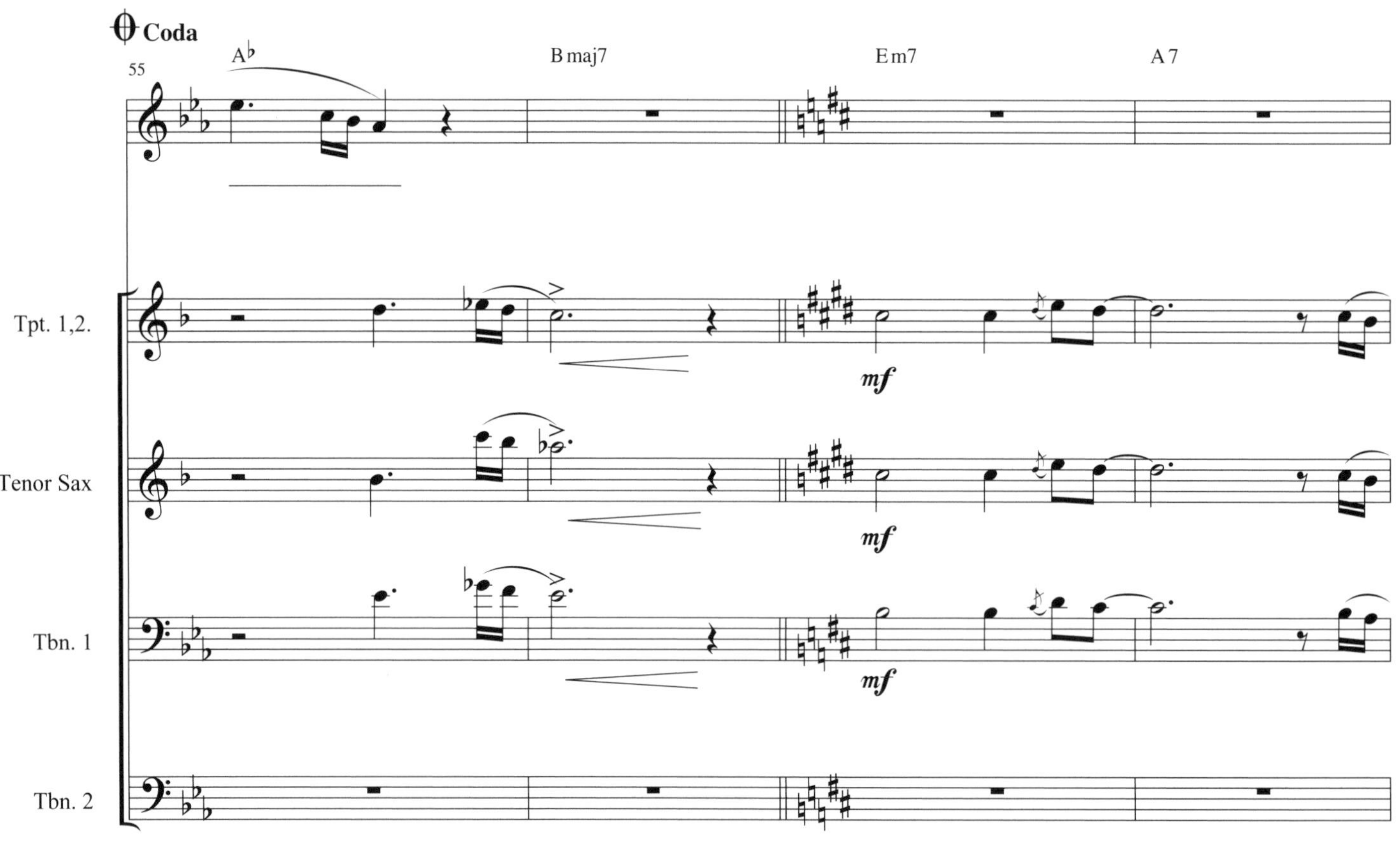
Coda
55
A♭
Bmaj7
Em7
A7
Tpt. 1,2.
Tenor Sax
Tbn. 1
Tbn. 2
mf

59
Em7
A7
Em7
A7
Tpt. 1,2.
Tenor Sax
Tbn. 1
Tbn. 2

63
Em7
A7
Em7
A7
Tpt. 1,2.
Tenor Sax
Tbn. 1
Tbn. 2

67
Em7
A7
Em7
Tpt. 1,2.
Tenor Sax
Tbn. 1
Tbn. 2

70
A7
Em7
A7
Tpt. 1,2.
Tenor Sax
Tbn. 1
Tbn. 2

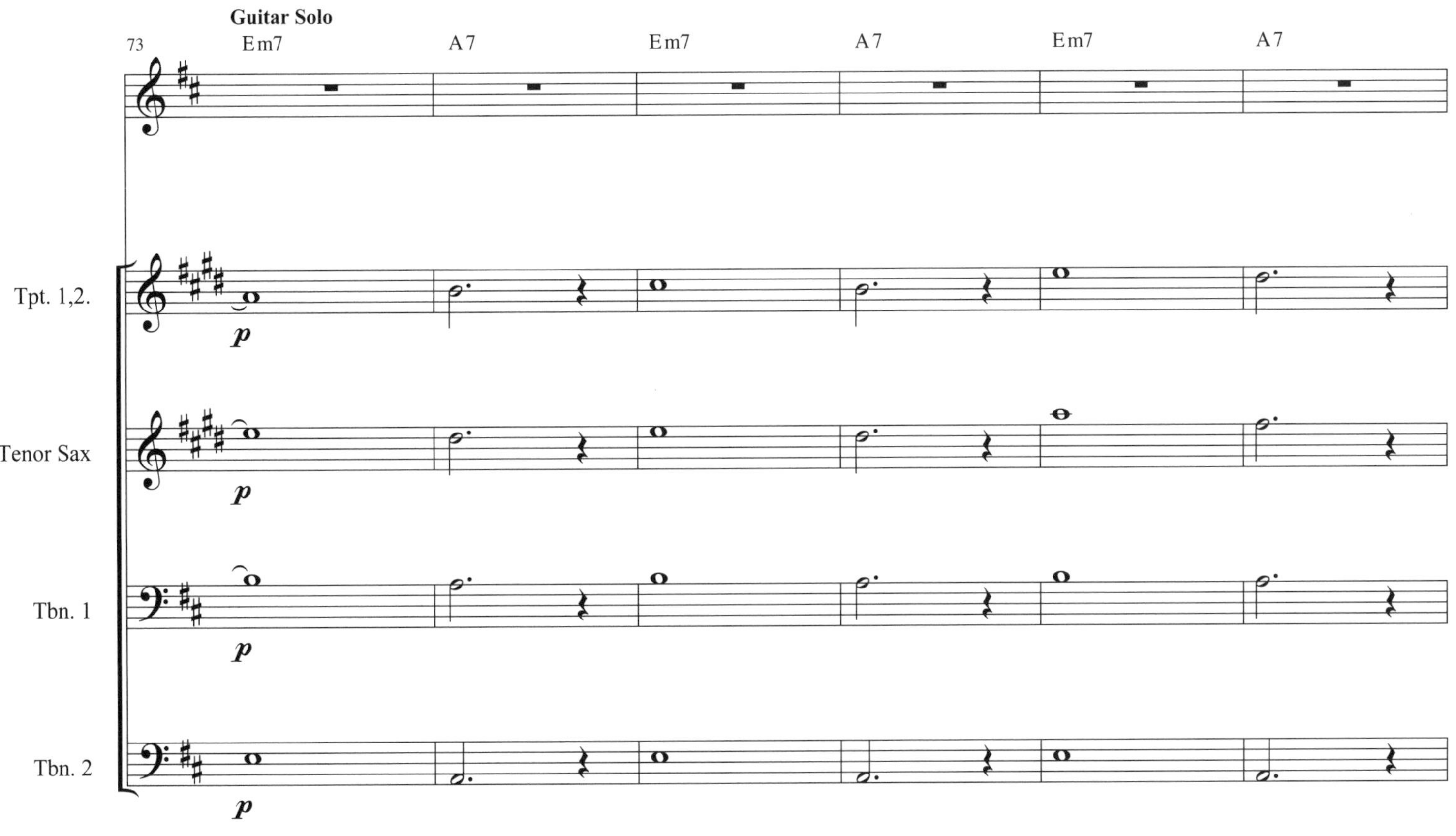
Guitar Solo
73
Em7
A7
Em7
A7
Em7
A7
Tpt. 1,2.
p
Tenor Sax
p
Tbn. 1
p
Tbn. 2
p

79
Em7
A7
Em7
A7
Tpt. 1,2.
mf
Tenor Sax
mf
Tbn. 1
mf
Tbn. 2

83
Em7
A7
Em7
A7
Tpt. 1,2.
Tenor Sax
Tbn. 1
Tbn. 2

87
Em7
A7
G sus
Tpt. 1,2.
p
Tenor Sax
p
Tbn. 1
p
Tbn. 2

91
B♭9sus
E♭
D♭
A♭
Now I need you
(Lead vocal ad lib.)
Tpt. 1,2.
Tenor Sax
Tbn. 1
Tbn. 2
f
mf

95
E♭
D♭
A♭
more than ev - er.
No more cry - in'.
Tpt. 1,2.
Tenor Sax
Tbn. 1
Tbn. 2

99
E♭
D♭
A♭
E♭
E♭/D
Cm
E♭
B♭sus
B♭
We're to - geth - er.
Tell me you will stay,
make me smile,
Tpt. 1,2.
Tenor Sax
Tbn. 1
Tbn. 2

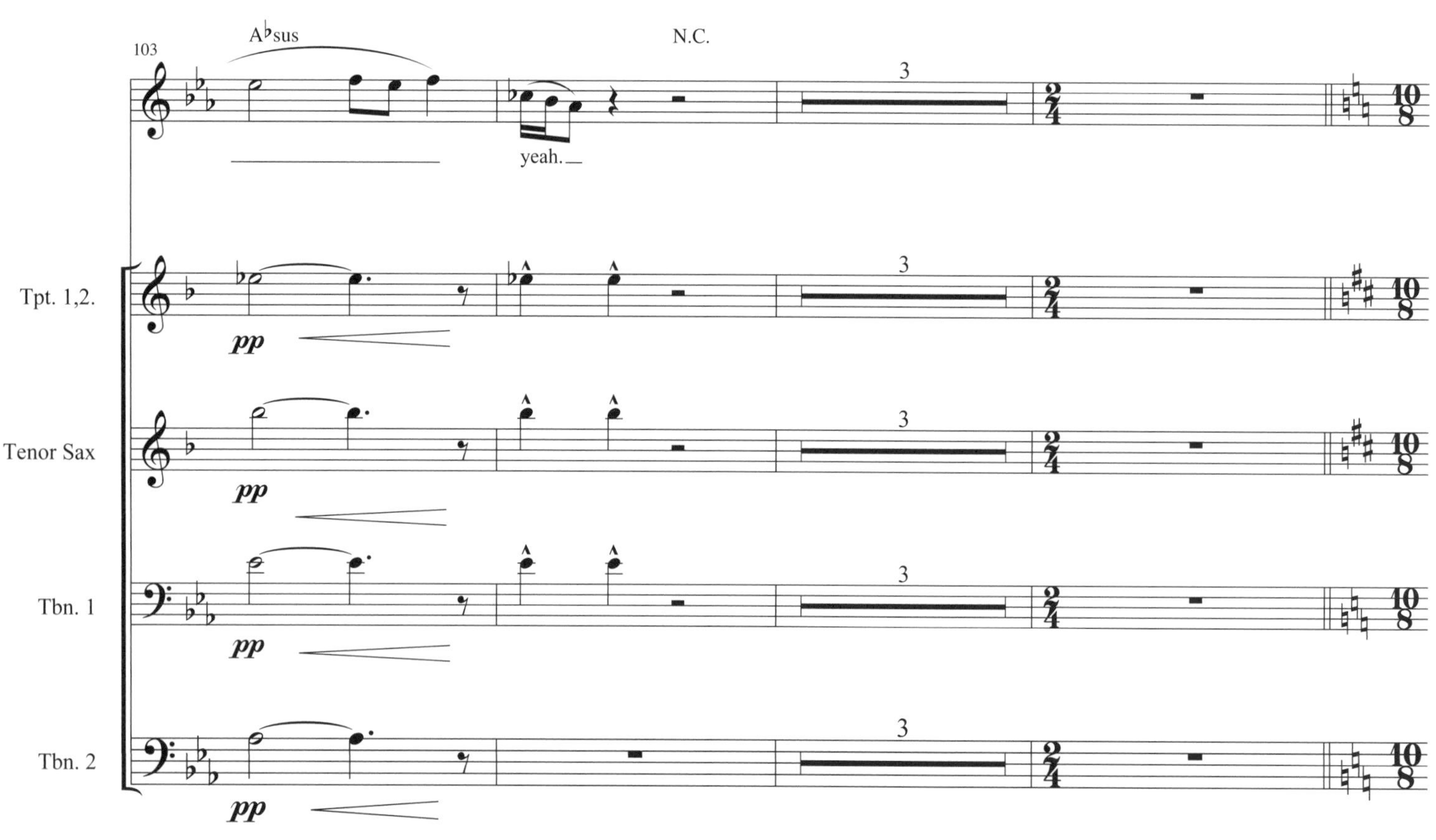
103
A♭sus
N.C.
yeah.
3
Tpt. 1,2.
Tenor Sax
Tbn. 1
Tbn. 2

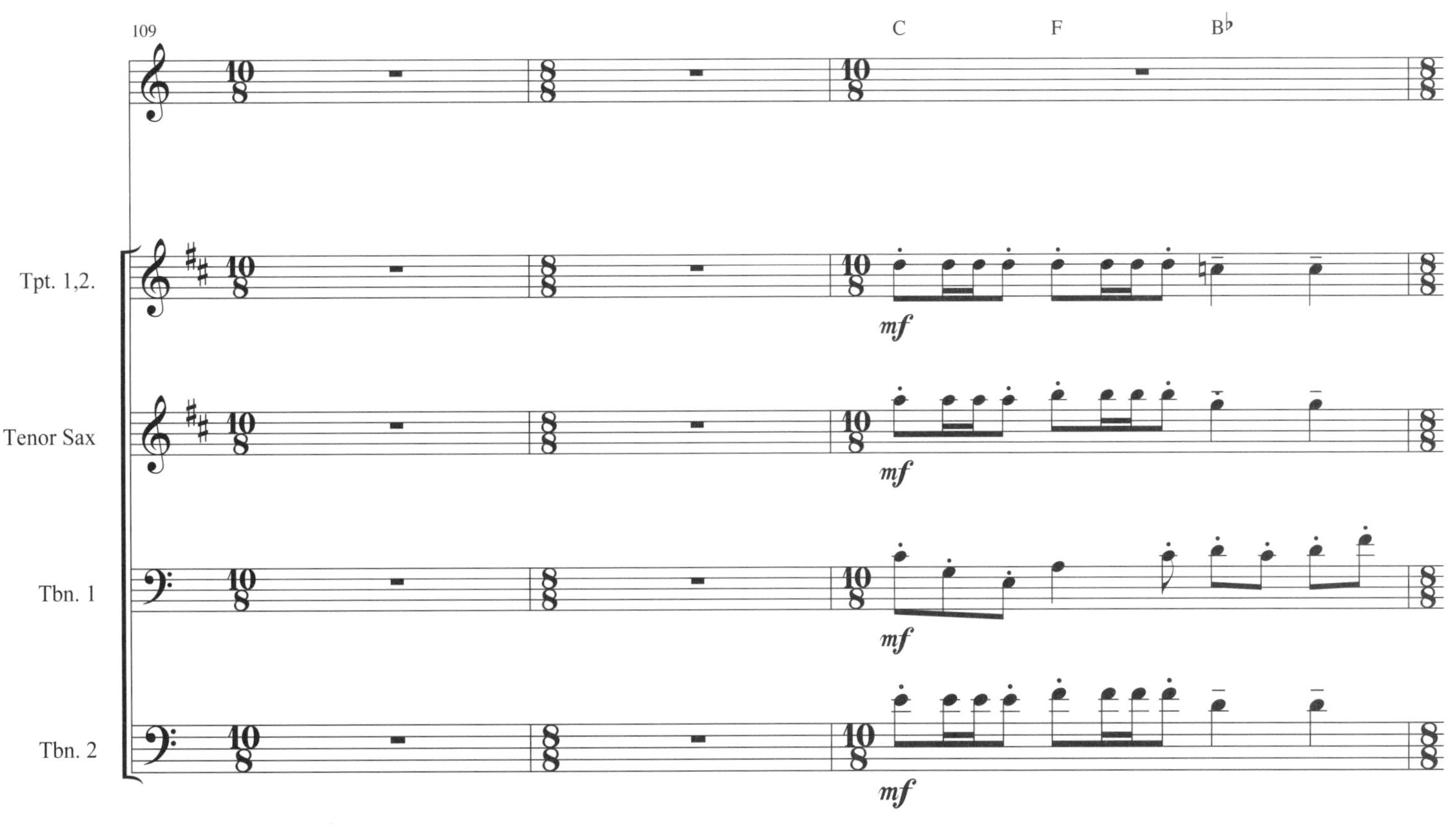
109
C
F
B♭
Tpt. 1,2.
Tenor Sax
Tbn. 1
Tbn. 2
mf

112
E♭sus
E♭
G
C
F
B♭
Tpt. 1,2.
Tenor Sax
Tbn. 1
Tbn. 2

114
E♭sus
E♭
G
C
F
B♭
Tpt. 1,2.
Tenor Sax
Tbn. 1
Tbn. 2

116
E♭sus
E♭
G
C
(Long hold, gradually crescendo)
Tpt. 1,2.
Tenor Sax
Tbn. 1
Tbn. 2
fp

MERCY, MERCY, MERCY

Composed by JOSEF ZAWINUL

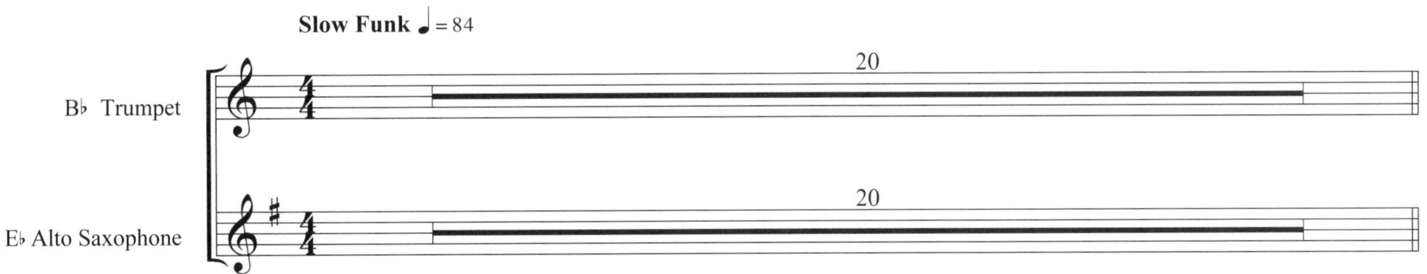

* *Chord symbols in this song are concert pitched.*

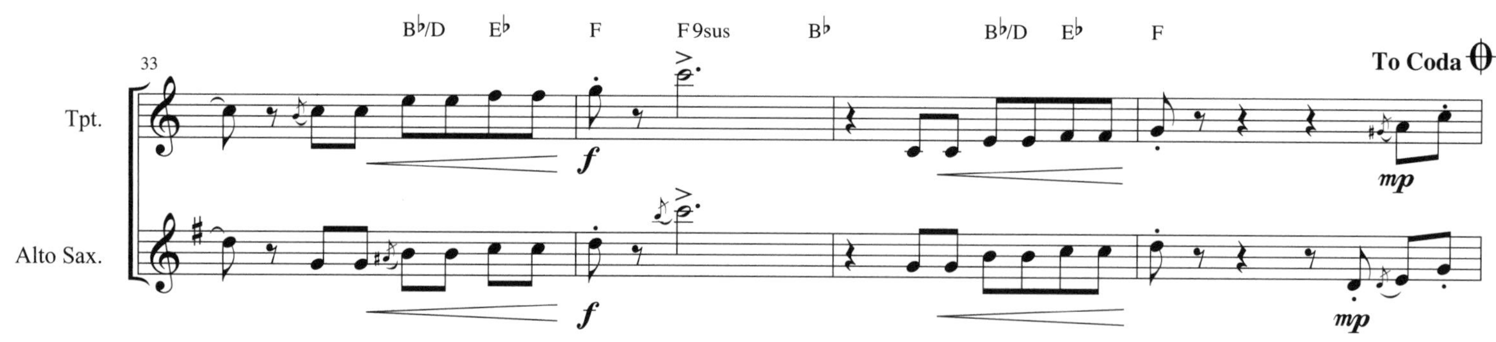
33
Tpt.
Alto Sax.
B♭/D
E♭
F
F9sus
B♭
B♭/D
E♭
F
To Coda
f
f
mp
mp

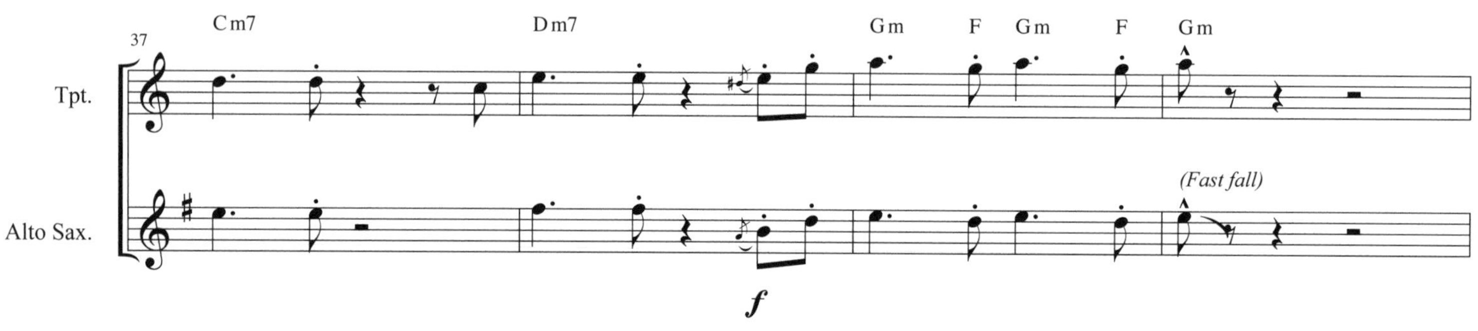
37
Tpt.
Alto Sax.
Cm7
Dm7
Gm
F
Gm
F
Gm
(Fast fall)
f

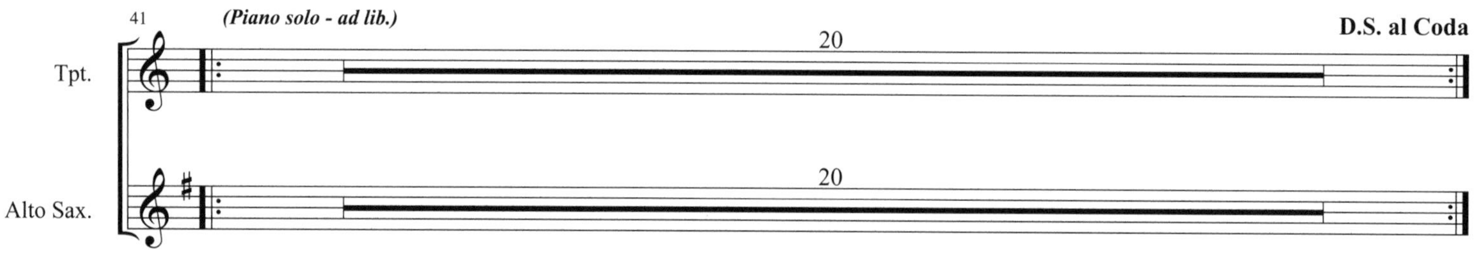
41
Tpt.
Alto Sax.
(Piano solo - ad lib.)
20
D.S. al Coda
20

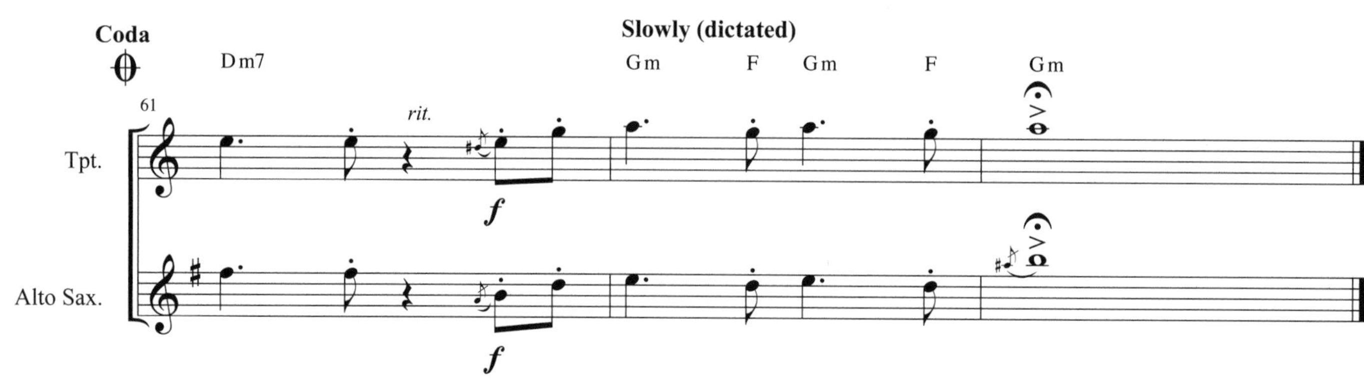
Coda
61
Tpt.
Alto Sax.
Dm7
rit.
Slowly (dictated)
Gm
F
Gm
F
Gm
f
f

PENNY LANE

Words and Music by JOHN LENNON
and PAUL McCARTNEY

6
Gmaj7
F♯7sus
F♯7
F♯7sus
F♯7
— stop and say hel - lo.
On the
Tpt. 1/
Picc. Tpt.
Tpt. 2,3.
Fl. 1/Picc.
Fl. 2,3.

9
B
B/A♯
G♯m7
B/F♯
E6/9
C♯m11
F♯7sus
F♯7
B
B/A♯
G♯m7
B/F♯
cor - ner is a bank - er with a mo - tor - car, the lit - tle chil - dren laugh at him be - hind his
Tpt. 1/
Picc. Tpt.
Tpt. 2,3.
To Flute
Fl. 1/Picc.
Fl. 2,3.

12
Bm
G♯m7♭5
Gmaj7
F♯7sus
F♯7
back. And the bank-er nev-er wears a mac in the pour-ing rain,
Tpt. 1/ Picc. Tpt.
Tpt. 2,3.
Fl. 1/Picc.
Fl. 2,3.

16
E
N.C.
A
A/C♯
D
ver-y strange. Pen-ny Lane is in my ears and in my eyes.
B♭ Trumpet
Tpt. 1/ Picc. Tpt.
Tpt. 2,3.
Fl. 1/Picc.
Fl. 2,3.
mf

20
A
A/C♯
D
There be - neath the blue___ sub - ur - ban skies___ I sit, and
To Picc. Tpt. in "A"
Tpt. 1/ Picc. Tpt.
Tpt. 2,3.
Fl. 1/Picc.
Fl. 2,3.

24
F♯7
N.C.
B
B/A♯
G♯m7
B/F♯
E6 9
C♯m11
F♯7sus
F♯7
mean - while back in Pen - ny Lane,___ there is a fire - man with an hour - glass, and in his pock -
Tpt. 1/ Picc. Tpt.
Tpt. 2,3.
Fl. 1/Picc.
Fl. 2,3.
mp
mp

27
B
B/A♯
G♯m7
B/F♯
Bm
G♯m7♭5
- et is a por - trait of the Queen.
He likes to keep his fire en - gine clean,
Tpt. 1/ Picc. Tpt.
Tpt. 2,3.
Fl. 1/Picc.
Fl. 2,3.
mf
mf

30
Gmaj7
F♯7sus
F♯7
F♯7sus
F♯7
it's a clean ma - chine.
Ah.
Tpt. 1/ Picc. Tpt.
Tpt. 2,3.
Fl. 1/Picc.
Fl. 2,3.
mp

33
B
B/A♯
G♯m7
B/F♯
E6 9
C♯m11
F♯7sus
F♯7
B
B/A♯
G♯m7
B/F♯
Ah.
Picc. Tpt. in "A"
Solo (Classical):
Tpt. 1/ Picc. Tpt.
Tpt. 2,3.
Fl. 1/Picc.
Fl. 2,3.

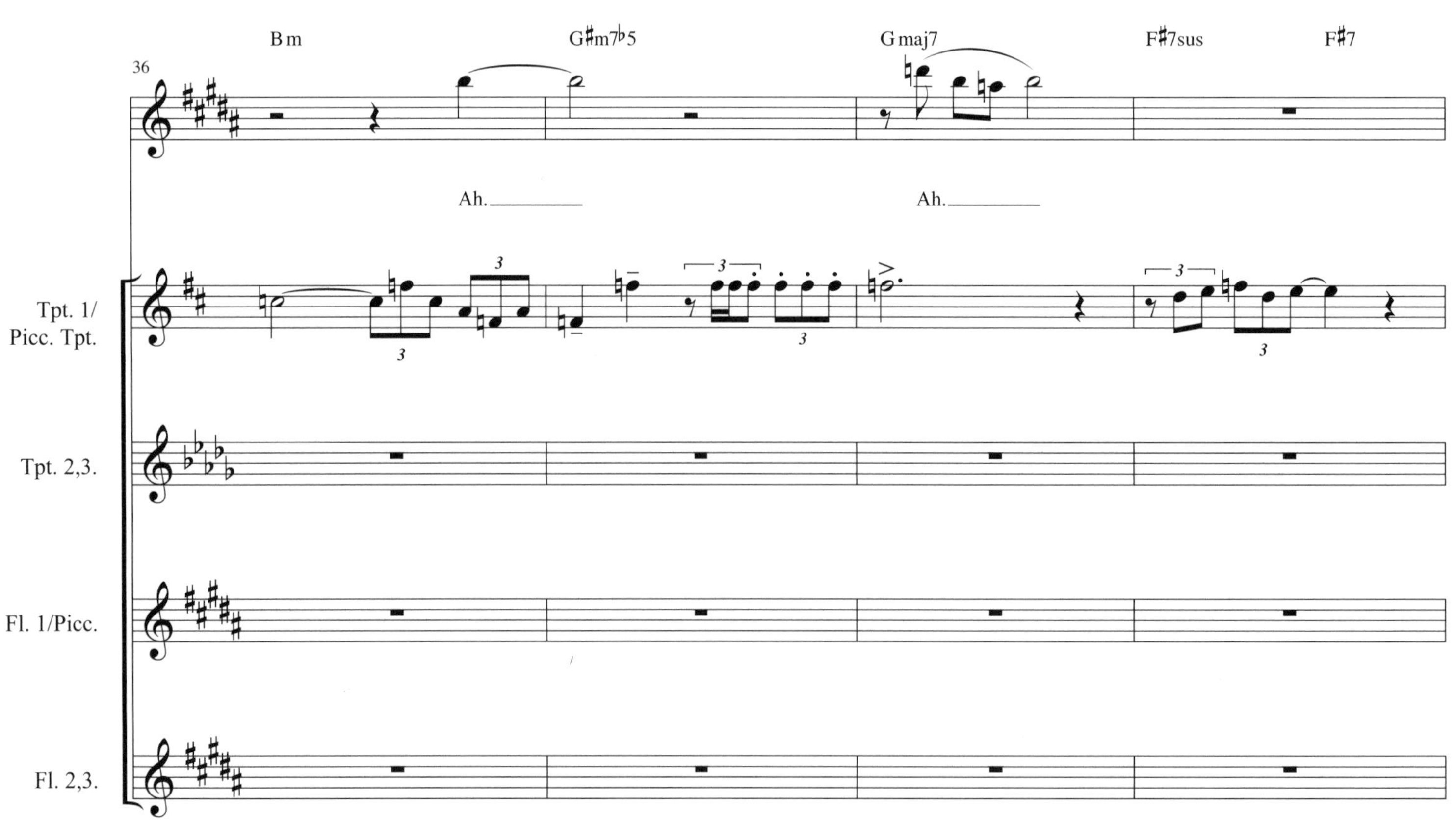
36
Bm
G♯m7♭5
G maj7
F♯7sus
F♯7
Ah.
Ah.
Tpt. 1/ Picc. Tpt.
Tpt. 2,3.
Fl. 1/Picc.
Fl. 2,3.

40
E
N.C.
A
A/C♯
Pen-ny Lane
is in my ears
and in my eyes,
To B♭ Trumpet
Tpt. 1/ Picc. Tpt.
Tpt. 2,3.
Fl. 1/Picc.
Fl. 2,3.

43
D
A
A/C♯
four of fish and fin - ger pies
Tpt. 1/ Picc. Tpt.
Tpt. 2,3.
Fl. 1/Picc.
Fl. 2,3.

47
D
F♯7
N.C.
B
B/A♯
G♯m7
B/F♯
in sum - mer. Mean - while back be - hind the shel - ter in the mid - dle of the round -
To Picc. Tpt. in "A"
Tpt. 1/
Picc. Tpt.
Tpt. 2,3.
mf
Fl. 1/Picc.
mp
Fl. 2,3.
mp

50
E9 6
C♯m11
F♯7sus
F♯7
B
B/A♯
G♯m7
B/F♯
Bm
a - bout, a pret - ty nurse is sell - ing pop - pies from a tray, and though she
Tpt. 1/
Picc. Tpt.
Tpt. 2,3.
Fl. 1/Picc.
Fl. 2,3.

53
G♯m7♭5
Gmaj7
F♯7sus
F♯7
F♯7sus
F♯7
feels as if she's in a play, she is an - y - way.
Pen - ny Lane,
Picc. Tpt. in "A"
Tpt. 1/ Picc. Tpt.
Tpt. 2,3.
Fl. 1/Picc.
Fl. 2,3.

57
B
B/A♯
G♯m7
B/F♯
E6 9
C♯m11
F♯7sus
F♯7
B
B/A♯
G♯m7
B/F♯
the bar - ber shaves an - oth - er cus - tom - er.
We see the bank - er sit - ting wait - ing for a trim,
Tpt. 1/ Picc. Tpt.
Tpt. 2,3.
Fl. 1/Picc.
Fl. 2,3.

60
Bm
G♯m7♭5
Gmaj7
F♯7sus
F♯7
and then the fire - man rush - es in from the pour - ing rain,
3
Tpt. 1/
Picc. Tpt.
Tpt. 2,3.
Fl. 1/Picc.
Fl. 2,3.

64
E
N.C.
A
A/C♯
D
3
ver - y strange. Pen - ny Lane is in my ears and in my eyes.
Solo:
mf
f
To Picc.
Tpt. 1/
Picc. Tpt.
Tpt. 2,3.
Fl. 1/Picc.
Fl. 2,3.

68
A
A/C♯
D
There beneath the blue sub - ur - ban skies I sit. And
Tpt. 1/ Picc. Tpt.
Tpt. 2,3.
Fl. 1/Picc.
Fl. 2,3.

72
F♯7
N.C.
B
B/D♯
mean - while back... Pen - ny Lane is in my ears and in my eyes.
Tpt. 1/ Picc. Tpt.
Tpt. 2,3.
Picc.
Fl. 1/Picc.
Fl. 2,3.

75
E
B
There be - neath the blue
(Straight 8ths)
f
Tpt. 1/ Picc. Tpt.
Tpt. 2,3.
Fl. 1/Picc.
Fl. 2,3.

78
B/D♯
E
B
sub - ur - ban skies.
Pen-ny Lane.
Tpt. 1/ Picc. Tpt.
Tpt. 2,3.
Fl. 1/Picc.
Fl. 2,3.

PROUD MARY

Words and Music by
JOHN FOGERTY

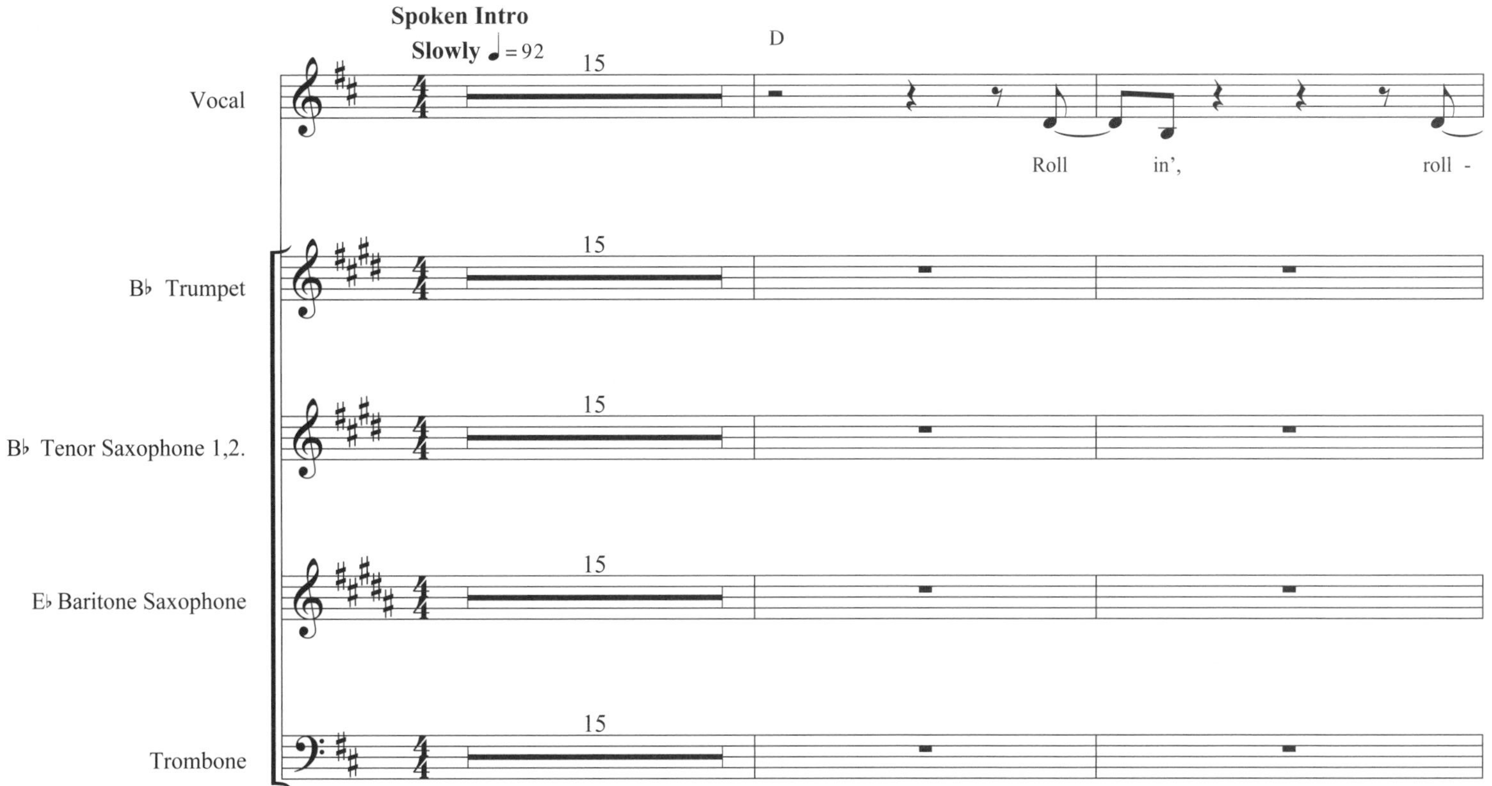

21
D
1. Left a good job in the cit y work-in' for the man ev - 'ry
2. (See additional lyrics)
Tpt.
Tenor Sax 1,2.
Bari Sax
Tbn.

24
night and day, and I nev er lost one min - ute of sleep - in'. I was
Tpt.
Tenor Sax 1,2.
Bari Sax
Tbn.

27
A
wor ryin' 'bout the way that things mighthave been.
Big wheel keep on turn -
Tpt.
Tenor Sax 1,2.
Bari Sax
Tbn.

30
Bm
G
- in', ooh, the Proud Mar - y keep on burn - in'. And we're roll -
Tpt.
Tenor Sax 1,2.
Bari Sax
Tbn.

33
D
1.
- in', roll - in', yeah, roll - in' on the riv - er. Cleaned
Tpt.
Tenor Sax 1,2.
Bari Sax
Tbn.

37
2.
D
rit.
in' on the riv - er. Said we're roll in', roll - in', roll-
Tpt.
Tenor Sax 1,2.
Bari Sax
Tbn.

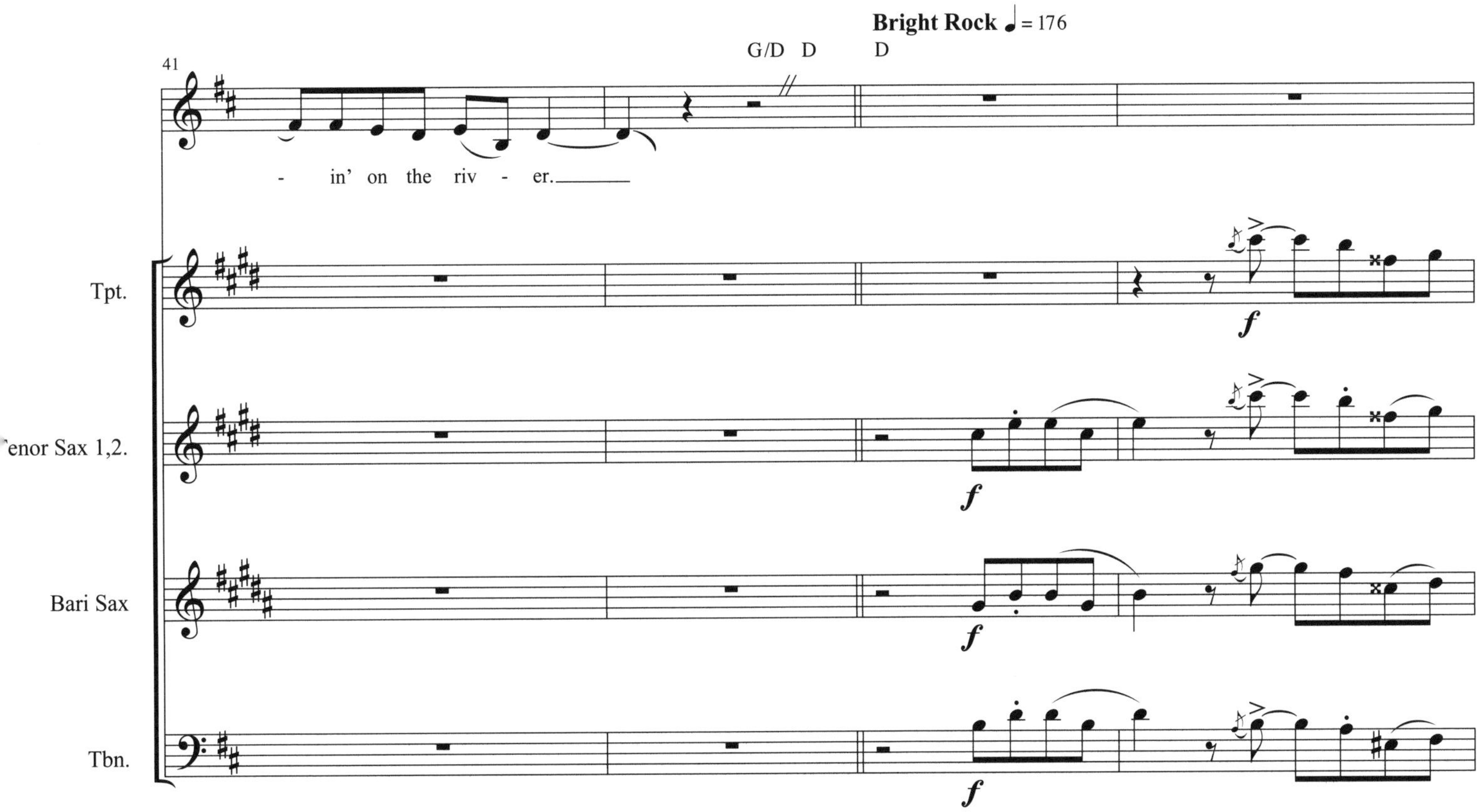
Bright Rock ♩ = 176
G/D D
D
41
- in' on the riv - er.
Tpt.
enor Sax 1,2.
Bari Sax
Tbn.
f

45
Tpt.
Tenor Sax 1,2.
Bari Sax
Tbn.

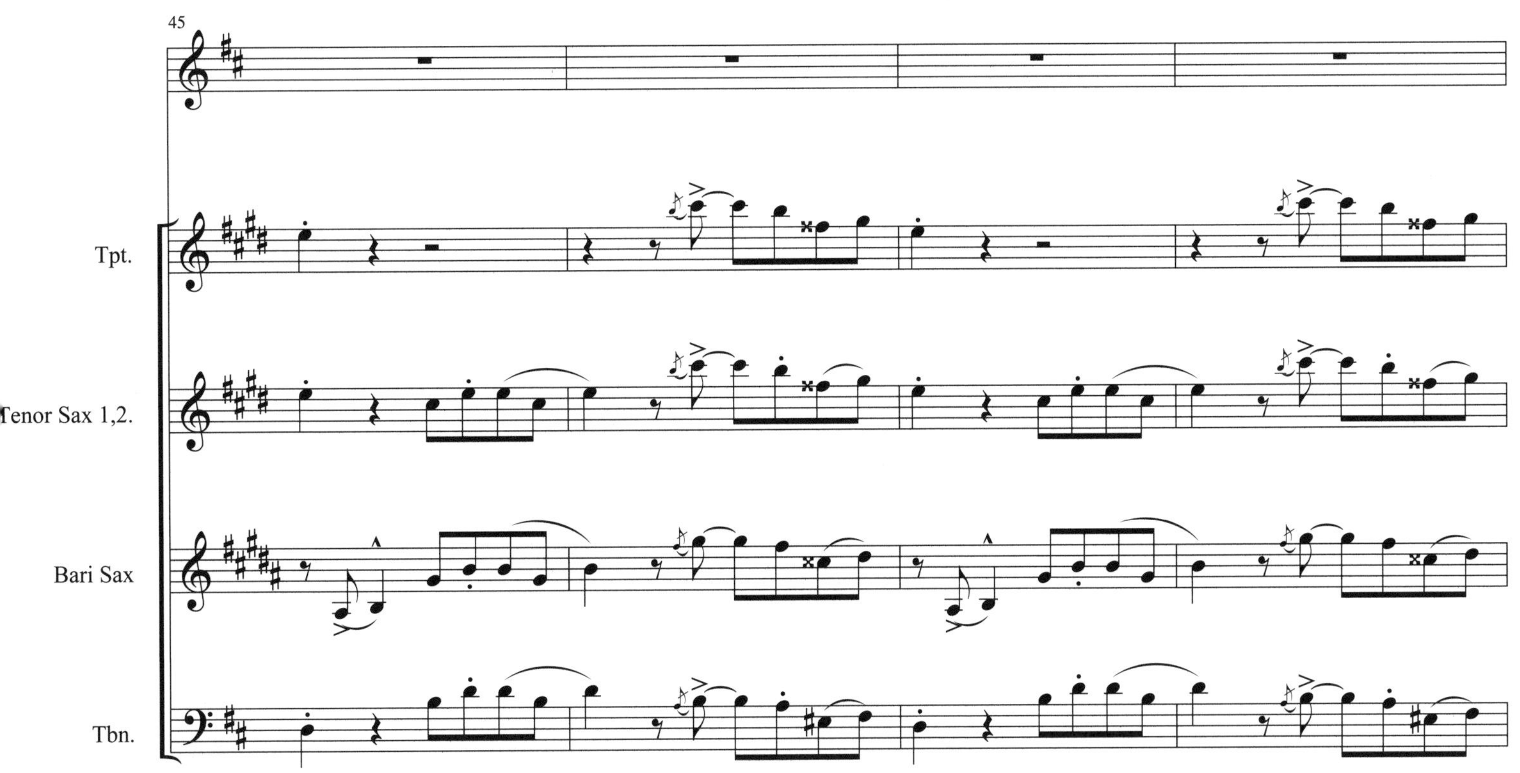

49
D
Well, I left a good job in the
Tpt.
Tenor Sax 1,2.
Bari Sax
Tbn.

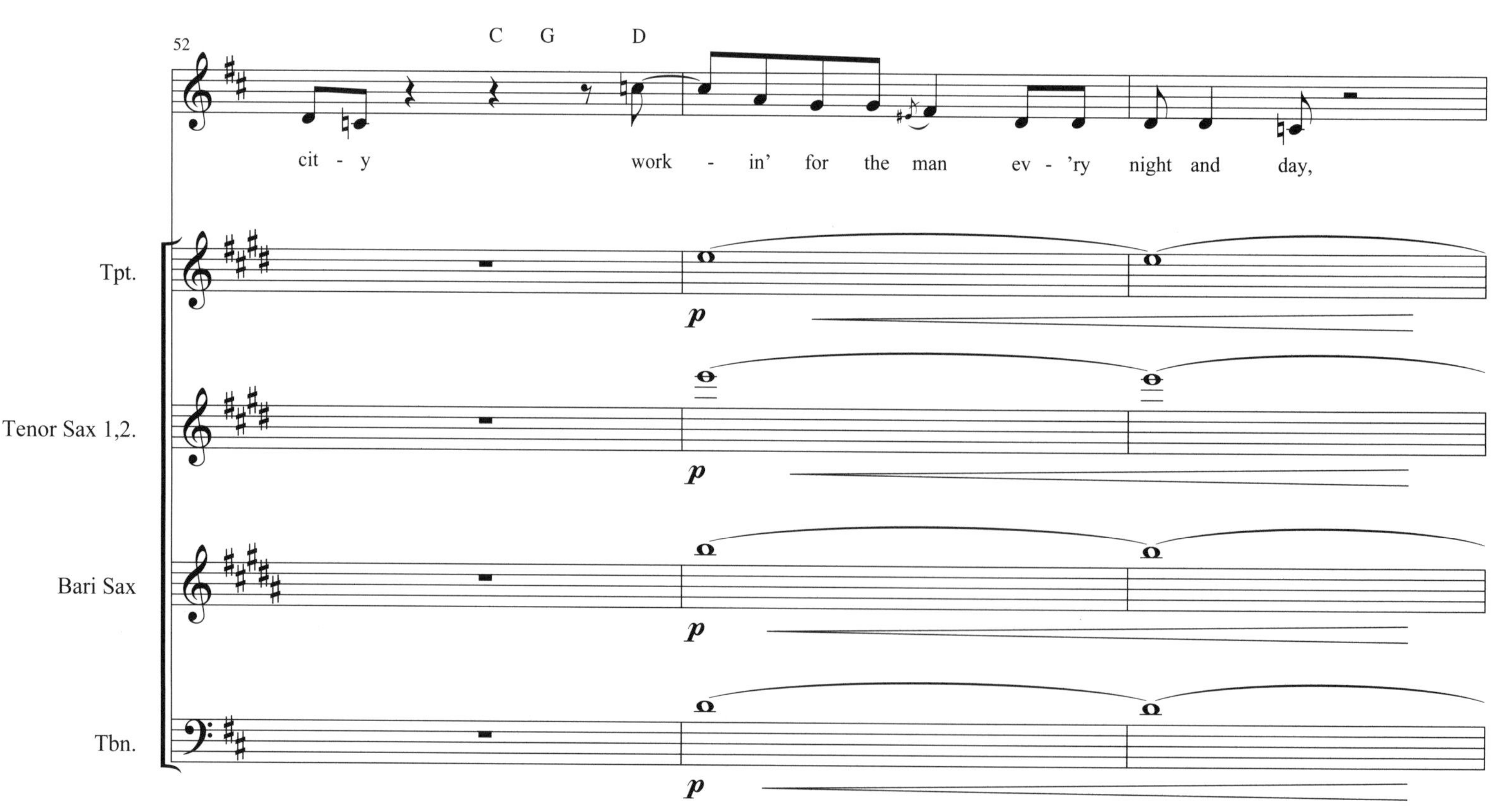
52
C G D
cit - y work - in' for the man ev - 'ry night and day,
Tpt.
Tenor Sax 1,2.
Bari Sax
Tbn.

55
and I nev - er lost one min - ute of sleep - in' wor - ryin' bout the way things
Tpt.
Tenor Sax 1,2.
Bari Sax
Tbn.

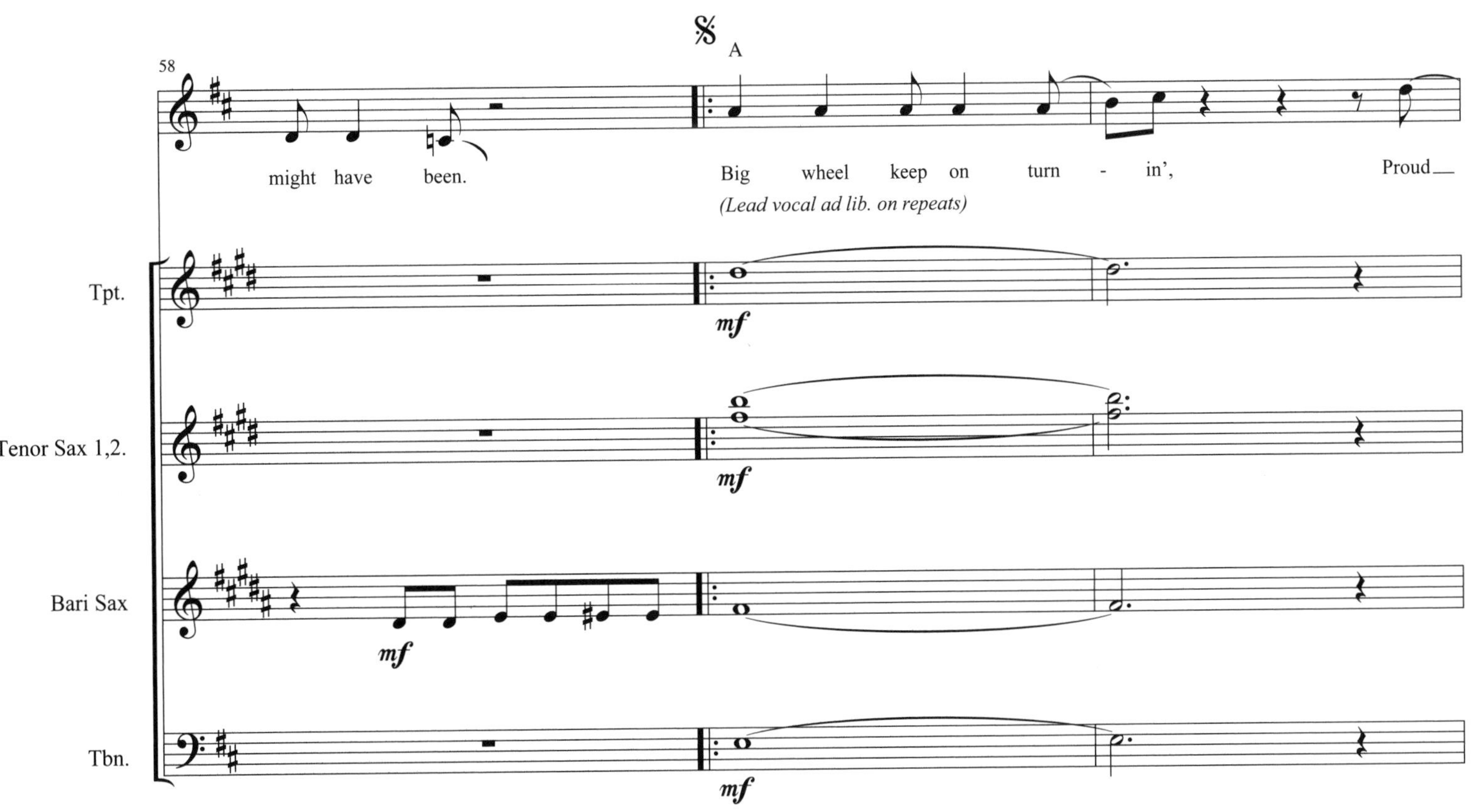
58
A
might have been.
Big wheel keep on turn - in', Proud
(Lead vocal ad lib. on repeats)
Tpt.
mf
Tenor Sax 1,2.
mf
Bari Sax
mf
Tbn.
mf

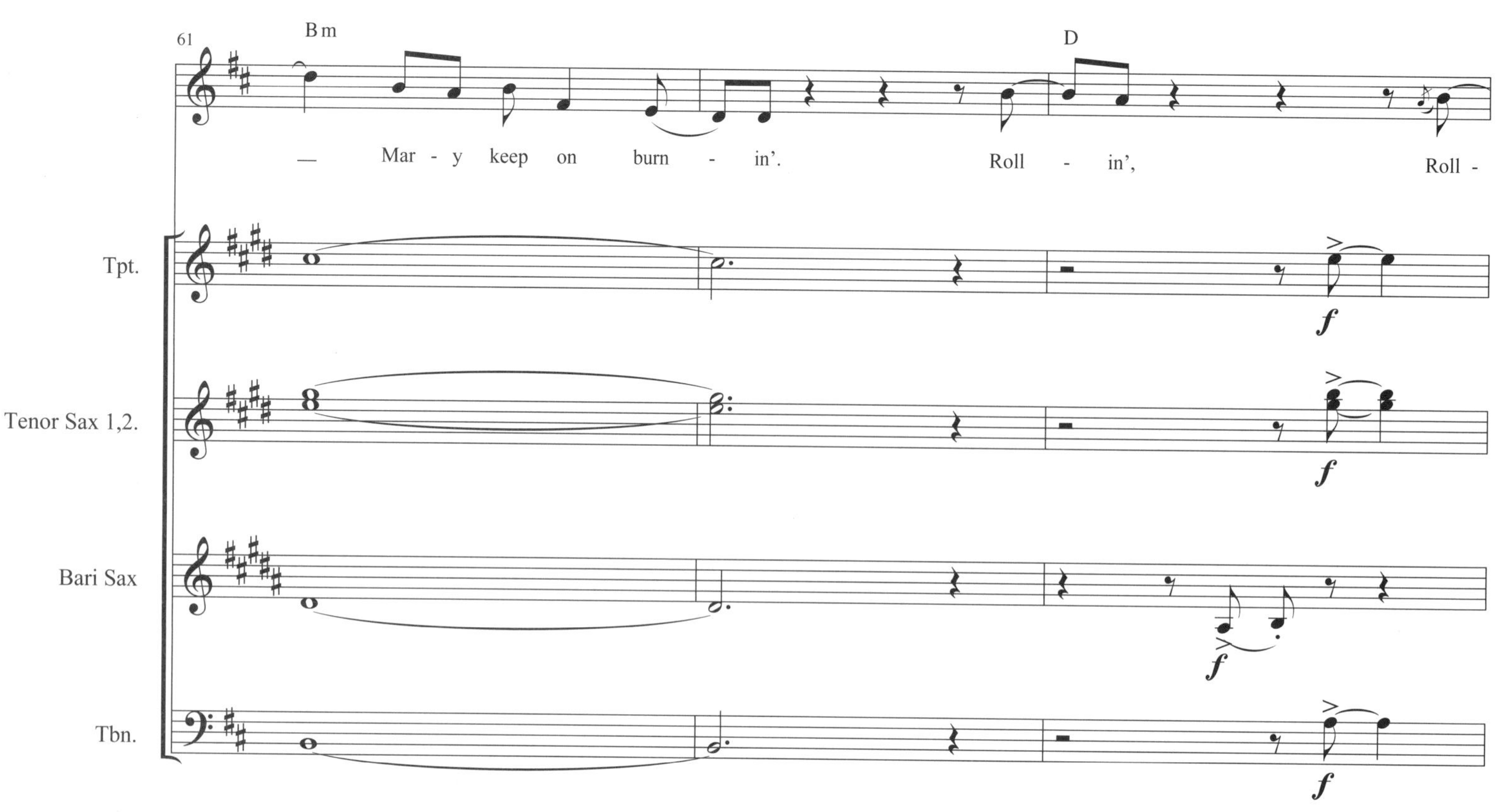
61
Bm
D
— Mar - y keep on burn - in'. Roll - in', Roll -
Tpt.
Tenor Sax 1,2.
Bari Sax
Tbn.

64
- in', roll - in' on the riv - er. Roll -
Tpt.
Tenor Sax 1,2.
Bari Sax
Tbn.

67
- in', said we're roll - in', roll - in' on the riv - er.
Tpt.
Tenor Sax 1,2.
Bari Sax
Tbn.

70
Doo-bop, doo, doo, doo, doo, doo, doo, doo, doo,
Tpt.
Tenor Sax 1,2.
Bari Sax
Tbn.

73
C
A
C
A
doo,
doo,
doo.
Tpt.
Tenor Sax 1,2.
Bari Sax
Tbn.

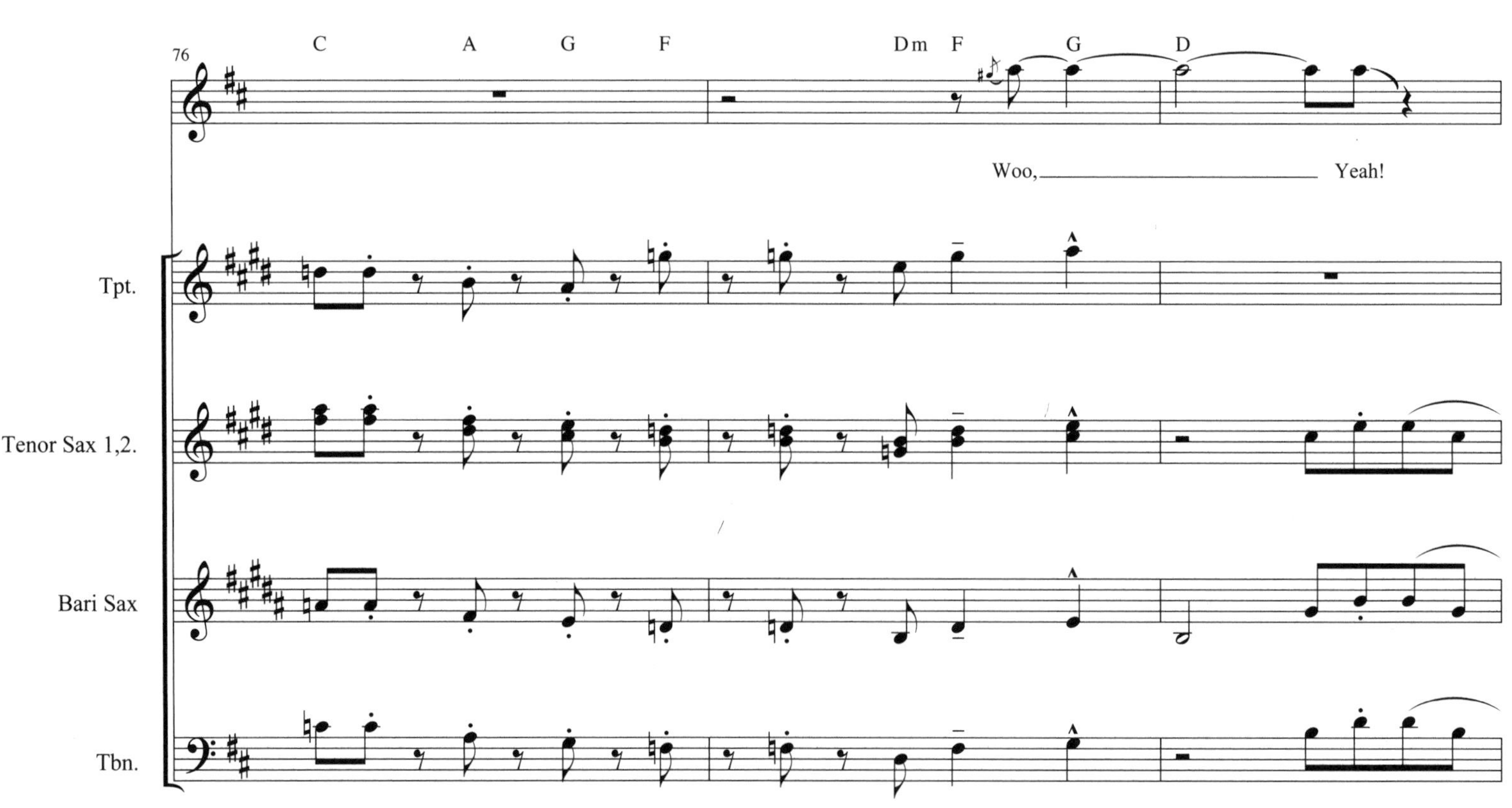
76
C
A
G
F
Dm
F
G
D
Woo,
Yeah!
Tpt.
Tenor Sax 1,2.
Bari Sax
Tbn.

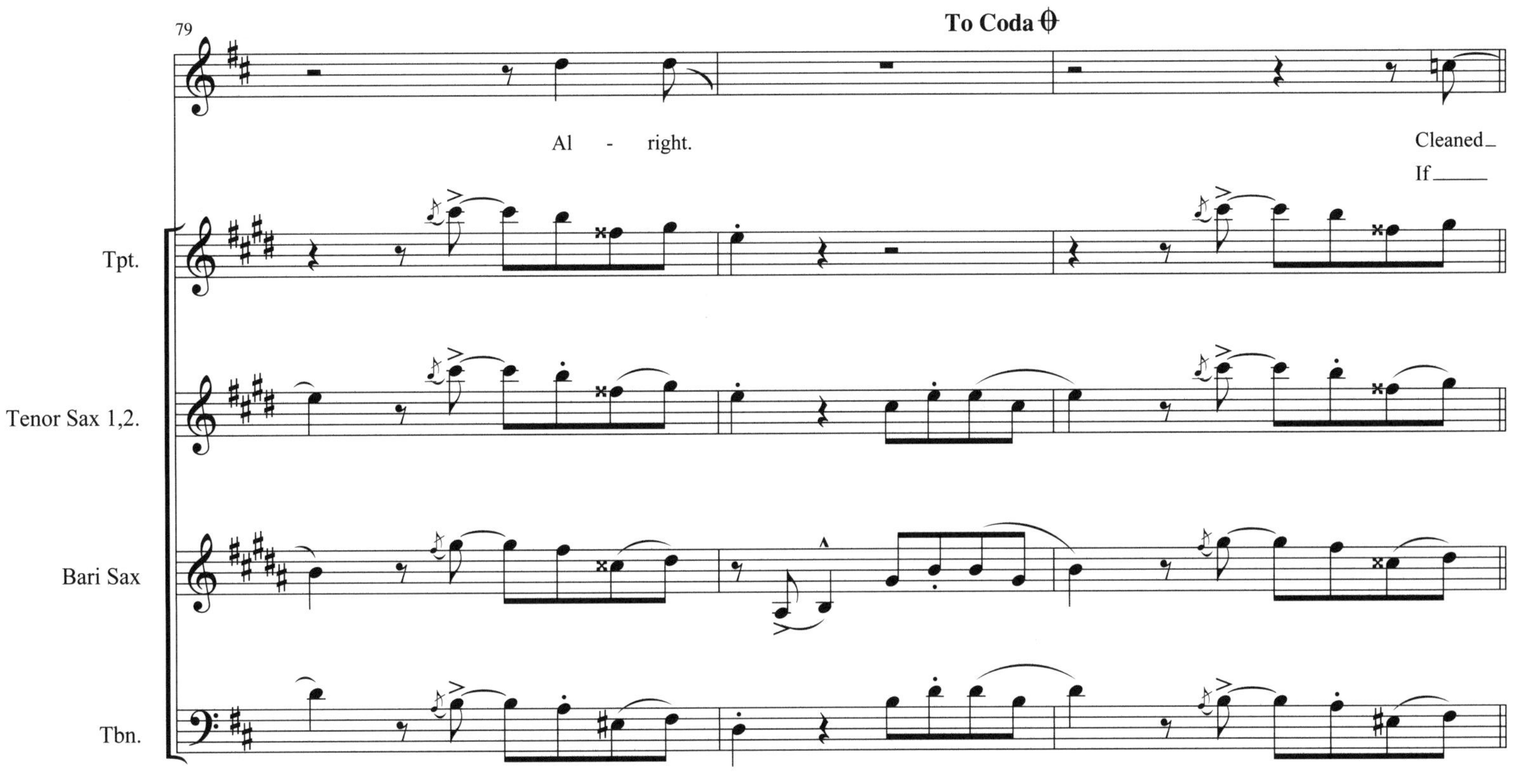

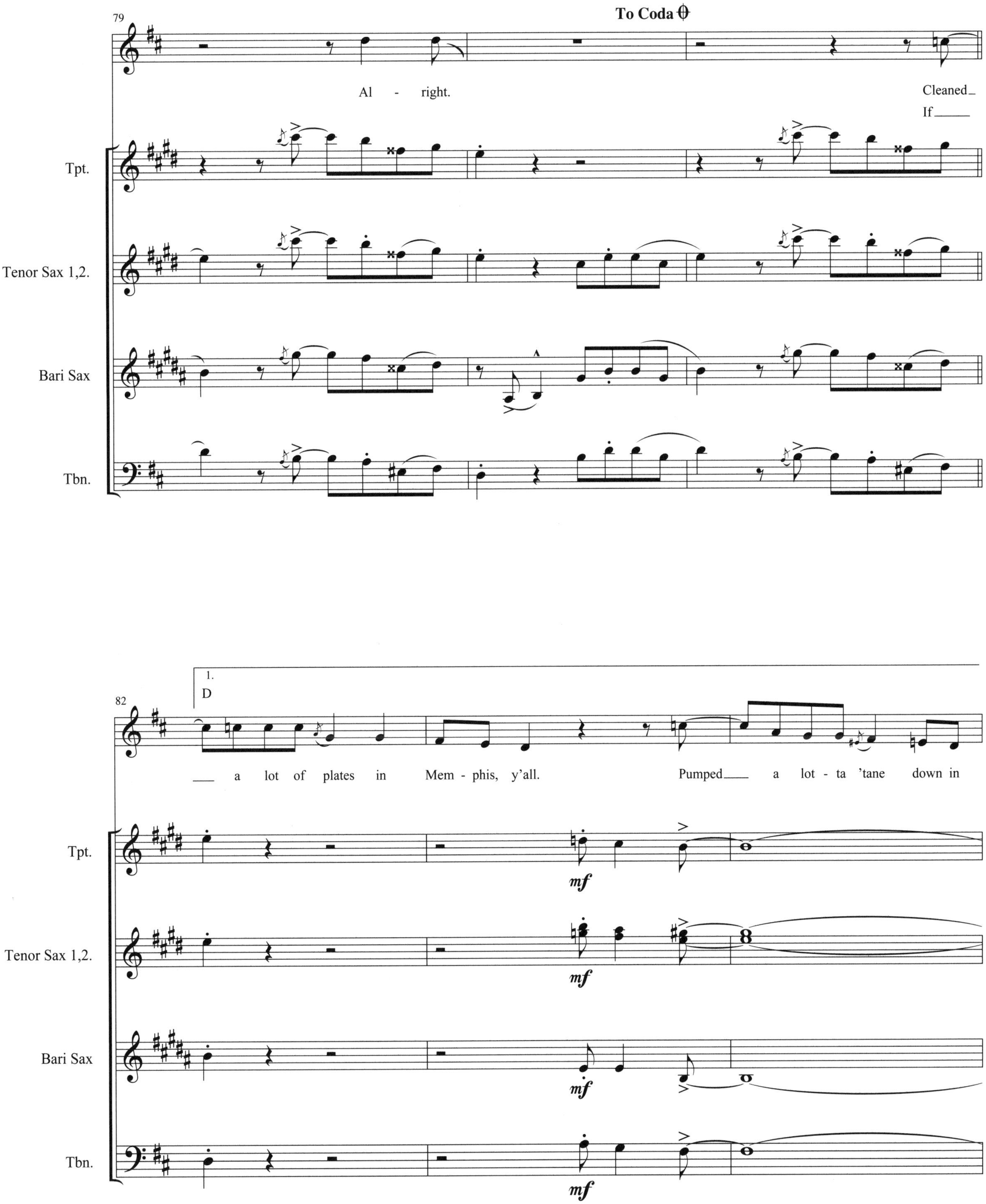

82
1.
D
a lot of plates in Mem - phis, y'all. Pumped a lot - ta 'tane down in
Tpt.
mf
Tenor Sax 1,2.
mf
Bari Sax
mf
Tbn.
mf

85
New Or - leans,
but I nev-er saw the good side of the cit - y 'til I hitched a ride on the
Tpt.
Tenor Sax 1,2.
Bari Sax
Tbn.

89
riv - er boat queen.
2.
D
you come down to the riv - er, well I bet
Tpt.
Tenor Sax 1,2.
Bari Sax
Tbn.
mp

92
— you're gon - na find some peo - ple who live.— You don't have to wor - ry if —
Tpt.
Tenor Sax 1,2.
Bari Sax
Tbn.

D.S. al Coda
95
— you got no mon - ey, the peo - ple on the riv - er are hap - py to give.—
Tpt.
Tenor Sax 1,2.
Bari Sax
Tbn.

Additional lyrics:

2. Cleaned a lot of plates in Memphis
   Pumped a lot of 'tane down in New Orleans,
   But I never saw the good side of the city
   Until I hitched a ride on the Riverboat Queen

SHAKE A TAIL FEATHER

Written by OTHA HAYES, VERLIE RICE and ANDRE WILLIAMS

8
G7
D
Bm
E7
So why didn't you ask me ba - by?
a Did - n't you think I could?
Tpt.
Tenor Sax
Bari. Sax
Tbn.
12
A
D
G7
Well I know that the Boo - ga - loo is out of sight, but the
mf

15
D
G7
D
Shing - a - ling's the thing to - night.
Well, if that was you and me out there, ba -
Tpt.
Tenor Sax
Bari. Sax
Tbn.
18
Bm
E7
A7
- by, I would - 've shown you how to do it right.
Do it right, uh-huh.
Tpt.
Tenor Sax
Bari. Sax
Tbn.

22
Do it right.
Do it right,
do it right.
Tpt.
Tenor Sax
Bari. Sax
Tbn.
28
D
G7
D
Aw,
twist it!
Shake it, shake it, shake it, shake it, ba - by.
Tpt.
Tenor Sax
Bari. Sax
Tbn.

33
A
G
D
Here we go Loop - de - loop.
Shake it out, ba - by.
Tpt.
Tenor Sax
Bari. Sax
Tbn.
38
G
A 7
Here we go Loop - de - li.
Bend ov - er, let me see you shake your tail - feath - er,
Tpt.
Tenor Sax
Bari. Sax
Tbn.

42
bend ov - er, let me see you shake your tail - feath - er, come on, let me see you shake a tail - feath - er,
Tpt.
Tenor Sax
Bari. Sax
Tbn.
46
1.
come on, let me see you shake a tail - feath - er. Aw,
Tpt.
Tenor Sax
Bari. Sax
Tbn.

50
2.
Play 16 times
D
1.-15.
G 7
Aw, come on.
Lead vocal ad lib.
See additional lyrics
Tpt.
Tenor Sax
Bari. Sax
Tbn.
54
16.
G 7
A 7
Aw,
Tpt.
Tenor Sax
Bari. Sax
Tbn.

Additional Lyrics:

(Come on)
Come on, baby.
Come on.
Yeah, come on, babe. Alright!
Do the Twist.
Do the Fly.
Do the Swim.
Ha, ha, ha. And do the Bird.
Well, do the Jerk.
Ah, do the Monkey.
Hey, Hey, Watusi.
And, ah, what about the Froog?
Do the Mashed Potato.
What about the Boogaloo?
Aw, the Bony Maroni.
Come on and do the Twist.
Out-Chorus

SO VERY HARD TO GO

Words and Music by STEPHEN KUPKA
and EMILIO CASTILLO

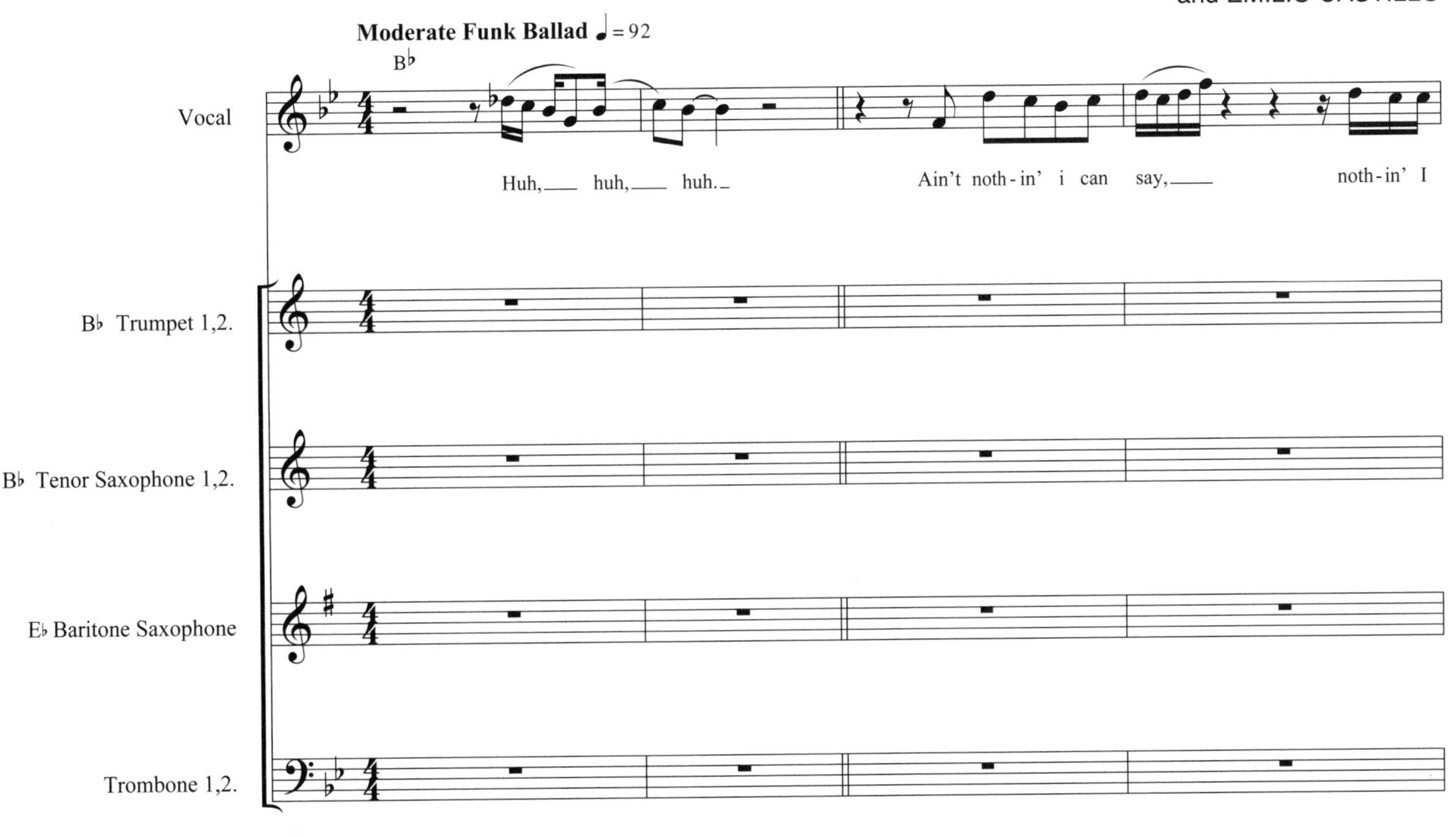

8
C dim7
B♭
I feel so blue.
Mmm.
Tpt. 1,2.
Tenor Sax 1,2.
Bari. Sax
Tbn. 1,2.

11
B♭
C 7
I got to make it right
for ev - 'ry-one con - cerned,
Tpt. 1,2.
Tenor Sax 1,2.
Bari. Sax
Tbn. 1,2.

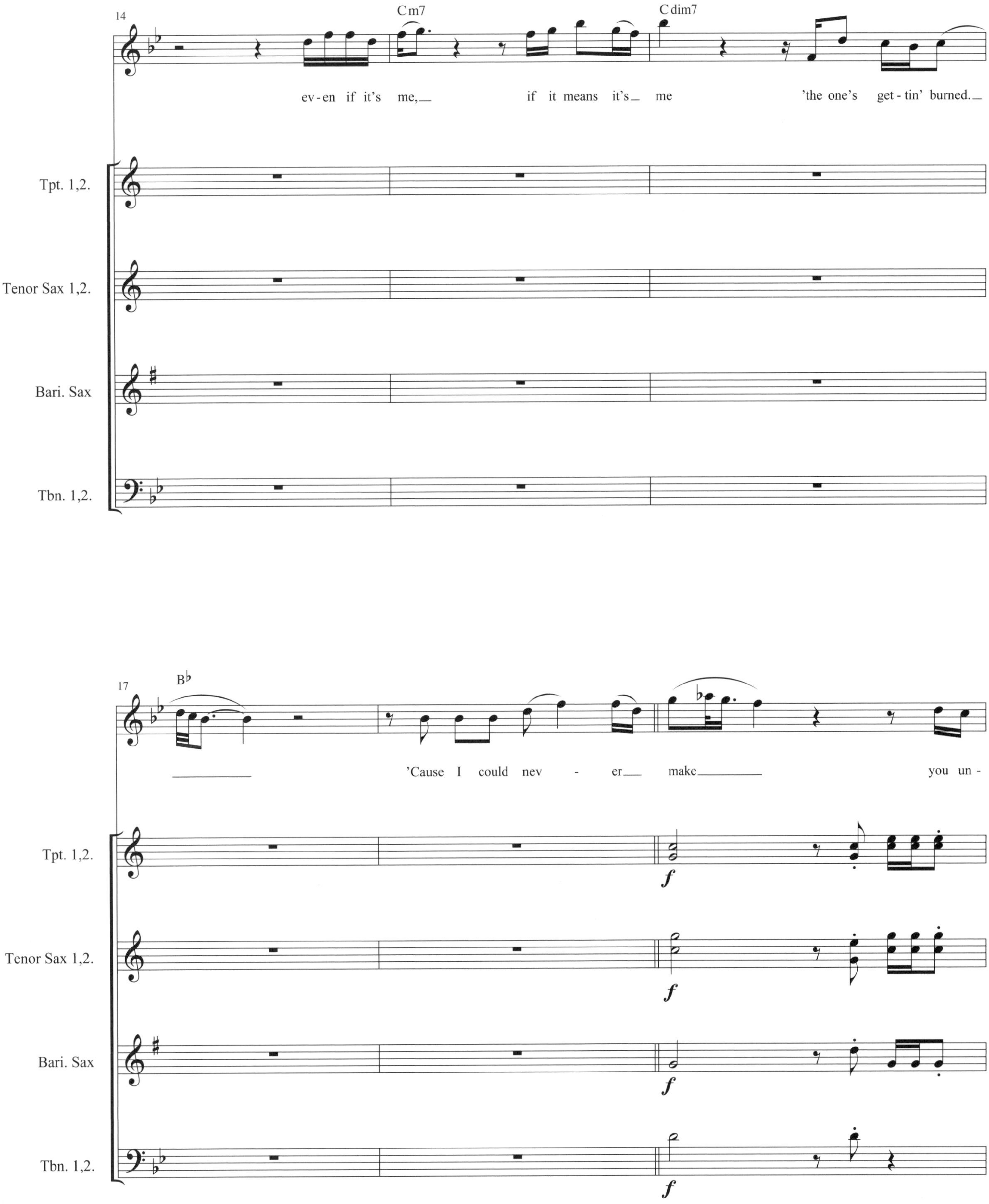

14
Cm7
Cdim7

ev-en if it's me, if it means it's me 'the one's get-tin' burned.

Tpt. 1,2.

Tenor Sax 1,2.

Bari. Sax

Tbn. 1,2.

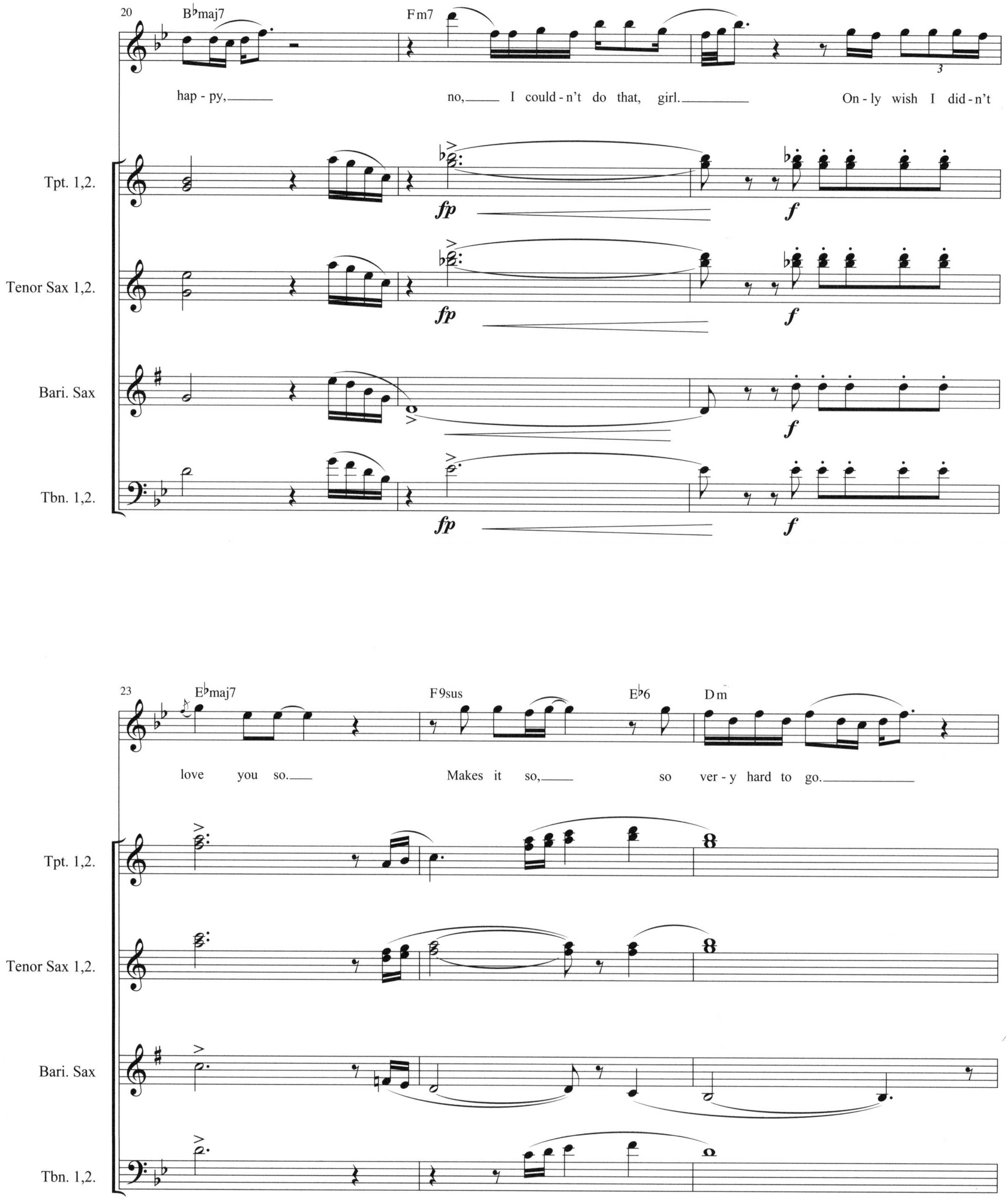

20 B♭maj7 Fm7

hap - py, no, I could - n't do that, girl. On - ly wish I did - n't

Tpt. 1,2.

Tenor Sax 1,2.

Bari. Sax

Tbn. 1,2.

fp f

26
F9sus
Gmaj9
C/D
(So ver - y hard to go.)
'Cause I love you so.
(So ver - y hard to
Tpt. 1,2.
Tenor Sax 1,2.
Bari. Sax
Tbn. 1,2.
29
Gmaj9
C/D
B♭
go.)
I, I love you so.
Huh...
Tpt. 1,2.
Tenor Sax 1,2.
Bari. Sax
Tbn. 1,2.

33
C7
I knew the time would come,
I'd have to pay for my mis-take.
3
Tpt. 1,2.
Tenor Sax 1,2.
Bari. Sax
Tbn. 1,2.

36
Cm7
Cdim7
I can't blame you for what you're do-in' to me, girl, ev-en though my
Tpt. 1,2.
Tenor Sax 1,2.
Bari. Sax
Tbn. 1,2.

39
B♭
heart aches.
Mmm.
Your dreams have all come true,
just the way you planned
Tpt. 1,2.
Tenor Sax 1,2.
Bari. Sax
Tbn. 1,2.

43
C7
them.
So I'll just step a - side,
Cm7
I'm gon' step
Tpt. 1,2.
Tenor Sax 1,2.
Bari. Sax
Tbn. 1,2.

46
C dim7
B♭
a - side, and lend a help - ing hand, then. 'Cause I could nev - er
Tpt. 1,2.
Tenor Sax 1,2.
Bari. Sax
Tbn. 1,2.
49
B♭
B♭maj7
Fm7
make you un - hap - py, no, I could - n't do that, girl.
Tpt. 1,2.
Tenor Sax 1,2.
Bari. Sax
Tbn. 1,2.
f
fp

52

E♭maj7 F9sus E♭6

On-ly wish I did-n't love you so. Makes it so ver-y hard to go.

Tpt. 1,2.

f

Tenor Sax 1,2.

f

Bari. Sax

f

Tbn. 1,2.

f

55

Dm F9sus Gmaj9 C/D

(So ver-y hard to go.)

'Cause I love you so.

Tpt. 1,2.

Tenor Sax 1,2.

Bari. Sax

Tbn. 1,2.

To Coda
Gmaj9
C/D
58
(So ver - y hard to go.)
8va
Hey!
Oh, I love you so.
Tpt. 1,2.
Tenor Sax 1,2.
Bari. Sax
Tbn. 1,2.
Flugelhorn Solo
61
B♭
C7
Ha...
C
D7
Tpt. 1,2.
Tenor Sax 1,2.
Bari. Sax
Tbn. 1,2.

D.S. al Coda
65
Cm7
Cdim7
B♭
Ha.
Huh.
I could nev - er
Dm7
Ddim7
C
Tpt. 1,2.
Tenor Sax 1,2.
Bari. Sax
Tbn. 1,2.
Coda
69
Gmaj9
C/D
(So ver-y hard to go.)
(So ver-y hard to
you so.
And it ain't eas-y to walk a-way when a man loves some-bod - y.
Tpt. 1,2.
Tenor Sax 1,2.
Bari. Sax
Tbn. 1,2.

Gmaj9
C/D
B♭
72
go.)
Hey!
Hey,
hey,
hey.
Tpt. 1,2.
Tenor Sax 1,2.
Bari. Sax
Tbn. 1,2.

SUBWAY TO VENUS

Words and Music by ANTHONY KIEDIS, FLEA,
JOHN FRUSCIANTE and CHAD SMITH

10
you're gon - na get it with the great - est of ease. Well, well, ev - 'ry - bod - y gath - er a - round.
Tpt. 1,2.
fp
Tenor Sax 1,2.
fp
Tbn. 1,2.
fp
12
All a - board the un - der - ground. You got - ta get in be - fore you get out,
Tpt. 1,2.
f
Tenor Sax 1,2.
f
Tbn. 1,2.
f
14
and get - tin' out is what it gon - na be a - bout. Well, if you find that you are blind,
Tpt. 1,2.
fp
Tenor Sax 1,2.
fp
Tbn. 1,2.
fp

16
Am7
o - pen up your bash - ful mind.
Let my band step in - side,
take you for a cos - mic ride.
Tpt. 1,2.
Tenor Sax 1,2.
Tbn. 1,2.
19
D7
E9
Let my band step in - side,
take you on a cos - mic ride.
Tpt. 1,2.
Tenor Sax 1,2.
Tbn. 1,2.
22
With
Tpt. 1,2.
Tenor Sax 1,2.
Tbn. 1,2.

25
hon-est sounds I'll paint your brain, for in this song I do pro-claim that once a-board this mov-ing train,_ I'll
Tpt. 1,2.
Tenor Sax 1,2.
Tbn. 1,2.
28
do my best to ease_ your pain. Slink-y as_ my speech may be, on this trip_ you'll ride_ for free,_
Tpt. 1,2.
Tenor Sax 1,2.
Tbn. 1,2.
31
Am7
as we leave_ our trail-er spots,_ where out-er space is not some pot. Ax-is bold as love, you see,_
Tpt. 1,2.
fp
f
Tenor Sax 1,2.
fp
f
Tbn. 1,2.
fp
f

34
D7
comes and goes so eas - i - ly.
Ax - is bold as love, you see,
comes and goes so eas - i - ly.
Tpt. 1,2.
Tenor Sax 1,2.
Tbn. 1,2.
37
E9
Tpt. 1,2.
Tenor Sax 1,2.
Tbn. 1,2.
40
Bm7
Space is king, or so I sing.
Tpt. 1,2.
Tenor Sax 1,2.
Tbn. 1,2.

43
1.
F C G
2.
F C G
A sub - way to Ve - nus. Ve - nus.
Tpt. 1,2.
Tenor Sax 1,2.
Tbn. 1,2.
f
f
f
46
E9
Tpt. 1,2.
Tenor Sax 1,2.
Tbn. 1,2.
49
Once a-board and feel-ing smooth,_ like the liq-uid you will ooze._ In -
Tpt. 1,2.
Tenor Sax 1,2.
Tbn. 1,2.
fp
fp
fp

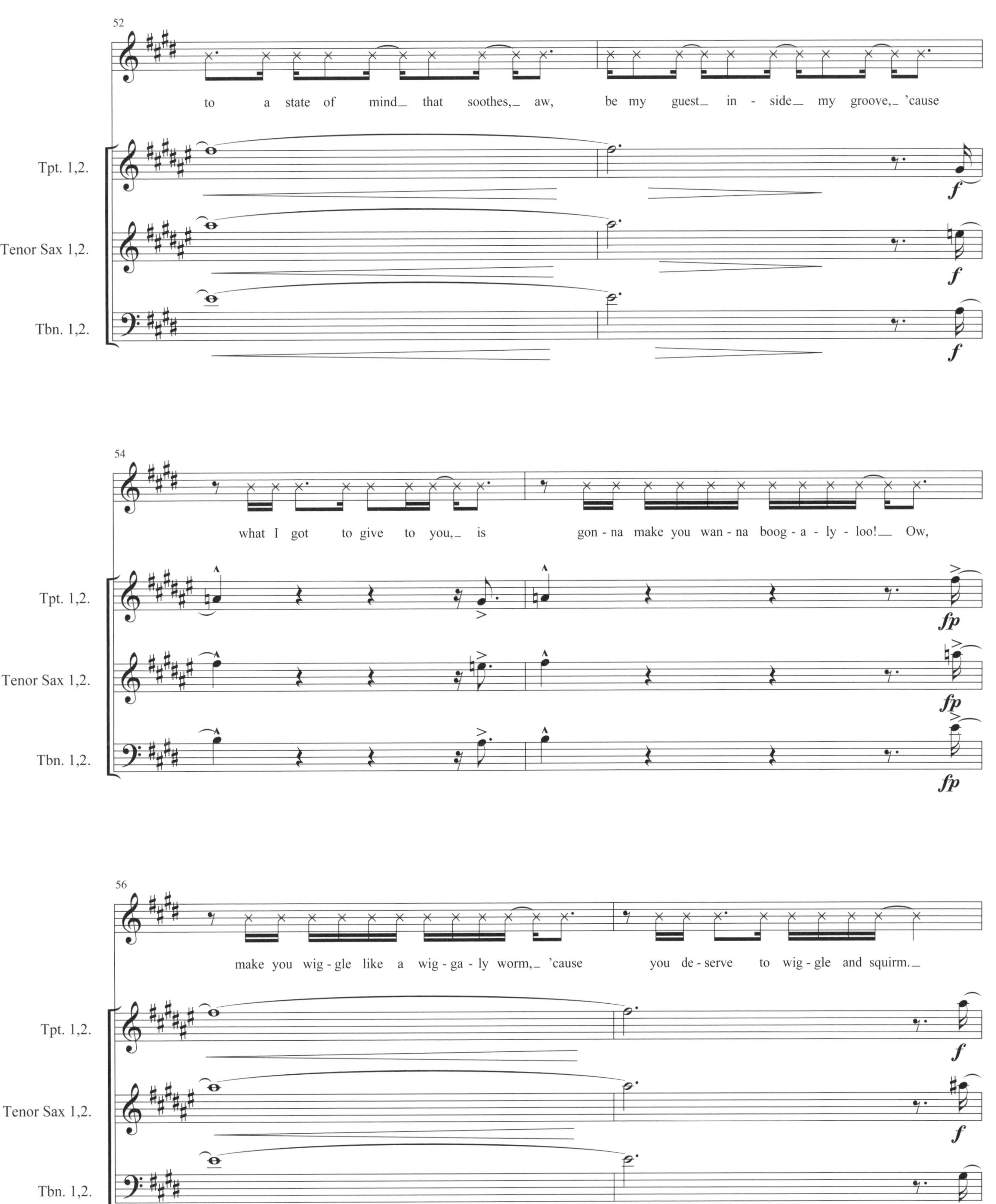
52
to a state of mind_ that soothes,_ aw, be my guest_ in - side_ my groove,_ 'cause
Tpt. 1,2.
f
Tenor Sax 1,2.
f
Tbn. 1,2.
f
54
what I got to give to you,_ is gon - na make you wan - na boog - a - ly - loo!_ Ow,
Tpt. 1,2.
fp
Tenor Sax 1,2.
fp
Tbn. 1,2.
fp
56
make you wig - gle like a wig - ga - ly worm,_ 'cause you de - serve to wig - gle and squirm._
Tpt. 1,2.
f
Tenor Sax 1,2.
f
Tbn. 1,2.
f

58
Am7
Life's too short to be in a hole,_ so bust in-to your funk-i-est stroll.
Tpt. 1,2.
Tenor Sax 1,2.
Tbn. 1,2.
60
D7
E9
Life's to short to be in a hole,_ so bust in-to your funk-i-est stroll!
Tpt. 1,2.
Tenor Sax 1,2.
Tbn. 1,2.
63
Tpt. 1,2.
Tenor Sax 1,2.
Tbn. 1,2.

66
Bm7
Space is king, or so I sing.
A sub - way to Ve - nus.
1.
F C G
Tpt. 1,2.
Tenor Sax 1,2.
Tbn. 1,2.
70
2.
F C G
Ve - nus.
4
Em7
76
Gm7
Ow!

79
E9
What I got to give to you__ is gon - na make you wan - na boog - a - ly - loo!__ Ow!
Tpt. 1,2.
Tenor Sax 1,2.
Tbn. 1,2.
81
make you wig - gle like a wig - ga - ly worm,_ 'cause you de - serve to wig - gle and squirm._
Tpt. 1,2.
Tenor Sax 1,2.
Tbn. 1,2.
83
Life's too short to be in a hole,_ so bust in - to your funk - i - est stroll. Well,
Tpt. 1,2.
Tenor Sax 1,2.
Tbn. 1,2.

85
shake your bod - y, a - shake it a - round,_ and do the dog on the ground,_ and
Tpt. 1,2.
Tenor Sax 1,2.
Tbn. 1,2.
87
if I can't make you dance,_ I guess I'll just have to make you piss your pants._
Tpt. 1,2.
Tenor Sax 1,2.
Tbn. 1,2.
89
B m7
Space is king, or so I sing._
(Lead vocal ad lib. 2nd time)
Tpt. 1,2.
(Horns tacet 1st time)
Tenor Sax 1,2.
(Horns tacet 1st time)
Tbn. 1,2.
(Horns tacet 1st time)

93
F C G
Bm7
A sub - way to Ve - nus.
Space is king, or so I sing.
Tpt. 1,2.
Tenor Sax 1,2.
Tbn. 1,2.
97
F C G
17
A sub - way to Ve - nus.
Tpt. 1,2.
17
Tenor Sax 1,2.
17
Tbn. 1,2.
17

Imagine playing the exact parts of some of the most memorable and consequential songs of our time note-for-note, exactly as the legends played them. This unique series features transcriptions of all the horn parts included on the original recordings.

FUNK/DISCO HORN SECTION

15 classics: Brick House • Disco Inferno • Dr. Funkenstein • Fire • Give It to Me Baby • Hold On I'm Comin' • Lucretia Mac Evil • Papa's Got a Brand New Bag • Pick up the Pieces • Serpentine Fire • Superstition • That's the Way (I Like It) • Y.M.C.A. • You Should Be Dancing • What Is Hip.

00001148 ....$19.95

POP/ROCK HORN SECTION

15 great hits: Bright Side of the Road • Higher Love • Hot Hot Hot • The Impression That I Get • Jump, Jive An' Wail • Livin' La Vida Loca • Magical Mystery Tour • Peg • Smooth • Spinning Wheel • Sussudio • 25 or 6 to 4 • Vehicle • Will It Go Round in Circles • Zoot Suit Riot.

00001149 ....$19.95

R&B HORN SECTION

15 R&B standards: Cut the Cake • Dancing in the Street • Gimme Some Lovin' • Hallelujah I Love Him So • Hard to Handle • I Got You (I Feel Good) • In the Midnight Hour • It's Your Thing • Knock on Wood • Mustang Sally • September • Sir Duke • Soul Finger • Soul Man • You've Made Me So Very Happy.

00001147 ....$19.95

JAZZ/POP HORN SECTION

15 jazzy favorites: After the Love Has Gone • Birdland • Deacon Blues • Doin' It (All for My Baby) • Fantasy • Got to Get You into My Life • Grazing in the Grass • In the Navy • The Madison Time • My Old School • Spanish Flea • Tell Her About It • Tijuana Taxi • What You Won't Do for Love • You Can't Get What You Want (Till You Know What You Want).

00001503 ....$19.99

JAZZ/ROCK HORN SECTION

14 rockin' gems: And When I Die • Does Anybody Really Know What Time It Is? • Feelin' Stronger Every Day • Get It On • Honky Cat • The Horse • The Letter • Make Me Smile • Mercy, Mercy, Mercy • Proud Mary • Shake a Tail Feather • So Very Hard to Go • Watermelon Man • Yellow Submarine.

00001504 ....$19.99

7777 W. Bluemound Rd. P.O. Box 13819 Milwaukee, WI 53213

www.halleonard.com

Prices, contents and availability subject to change without notice.

0112

Transcribed Scores are vocal and instrumental arrangements of music from some of the greatest groups in music. These excellent publications feature transcribed parts for lead vocals, lead guitar, rhythm, guitar, bass, drums, and all of the various instruments used in each specific recording session. All songs are arranged exactly the way the artists recorded them.

00672527	**Audioslave**	$24.95
00673228	**The Beatles – Complete Scores** (Boxed Set)	$85.00
00672378	**The Beatles – Transcribed Scores**	$24.95
00673208	**Best of Blood, Sweat & Tears**	$19.95
00690636	**Best of Bluegrass**	$24.95
00672367	**Chicago – Volume 1**	$24.95
00672368	**Chicago – Volume 2**	$24.95
00672452	**Miles Davis – Birth of the Cool**	$24.95
00672460	**Miles Davis – Kind of Blue (Sketch Scores)**	$19.95
00672502	**Deep Purple – Greatest Hits**	$24.95
00672427	**Ben Folds Five – Selections from Naked Baby Photos**	$19.95
00672428	**Ben Folds Five – Whatever and Ever, Amen**	$19.95
00001333	**Getz/Gilberto**	$19.99
00672540	**Best of Good Charlotte**	$24.95
00672396	**The Don Grolnick Collection**	$17.95
02500361	**Guns N' Roses Greatest Hits**	$24.95
00672308	**Jimi Hendrix – Are You Experienced?**	$29.95
00672345	**Jimi Hendrix – Axis Bold As Love**	$29.95
00672313	**Jimi Hendrix – Band of Gypsys**	$29.95
00672397	**Jimi Hendrix – Experience Hendrix**	$29.95
00672500	**Best of Incubus**	$24.95
00672469	**Billy Joel Collection**	$24.95
00672415	**Eric Johnson – Ah Via Musicom**	$24.95
00672465	**John Lennon – Imagine**	$24.95
00672478	**The Best of Megadeth**	$24.95
02500424	**Best of Metallica**	$24.95
00672541	**Pat Metheny Group – The Way Up**	$19.95
02500883	**Mr. Big – Lean into It**	$24.95
00672504	**Gary Moore – Greatest Hits**	$24.95
00690582	**Nickel Creek – Nickel Creek**	$19.95
00690586	**Nickel Creek – This Side**	$19.95
00672545	**Nickel Creek – Why Should The Fire Die?**	$19.95
00672518	**Nirvana**	$24.95
00672403	**Nirvana – In Utero**	$24.95
00672404	**Nirvana – Incesticide**	$24.95
00672402	**Nirvana – Nevermind**	$24.95
00672405	**Nirvana – Unplugged in New York**	$24.95
00672466	**The Offspring – Americana**	$24.95
00672501	**The Police – Greatest Hits**	$24.95
00672538	**The Best of Queen**	$24.95
00672400	**Red Hot Chili Peppers – Blood Sugar Sex Magik**	$24.95
00672515	**Red Hot Chili Peppers – By the Way**	$24.95
00672456	**Red Hot Chili Peppers – Californication**	$24.95
00672536	**Red Hot Chili Peppers – Greatest Hits**	$24.95
00672422	**Red Hot Chili Peppers – Mother's Milk**	$24.95
00672551	**Red Hot Chili Peppers – Stadium Arcadium**	$49.95
00672408	**Rolling Stones – Exile on Main Street**	$24.95
00672360	**Santana's Greatest Hits**	$26.95
02500283	**Joe Satriani – Greatest Hits**	$24.95
00672522	**The Best of Slipknot**	$24.99
00675170	**The Best of Spyro Gyra**	$18.95
00675200	**The Best of Steely Dan**	$19.95
00672521	**Best of SUM 41**	$29.95
00675520	**Best of Weather Report**	$18.95

Prices, content, and availability subject to change without notice.

For More Information, See Your Local Music Dealer,
Or Write To:

HAL•LEONARD®
CORPORATION

7777 W. Bluemound Rd. P.O.Box 13819 Milwaukee, WI 53213

Visit Hal Leonard online at **www.halleonard.com**

0212